Foreword

"Divine Appointment".

Meeting someone that becomes life changing in the ER on a cold, New England evening is not usually the beginning of an amazing relationship, but for us it was. My husband, Jimmy, was working late that evening and in a chance moment, met Pastor Dee (Skip Gunn's wife) and her girl. The concerned mom and her pained adult daughter were needing some answers and Jimmy was the tech that greeted them and made them feel taken care of through the process. In just a few minutes of conversation, my prayers were answered. The Lord had provided a church home for us while doing contract work in Massachusetts.

Since both of us were from the south, I think we were born again from the moment we were born. We didn't know anyone who didn't, at least know the gospel of Christ, much rather someone who didn't go to church most Sunday's (but many that certainly didn't live by the basic principles of a Christ follower). Some of those that I would have considered "mature" believers, rarely walked out their faith in a tangible way except in the occasional convenient ladies meeting, church offering or potluck dish. Certainly there were the "Christian" boycotts and play groups at the local Chick-fil-A and a coffee with a hurting friend once a year, if you couldn't get out of it. I was becoming like that too. We were dry. We certainly weren't the "on fire, world-changer, atmosphere shifters, doing greater works" kind of people, we wanted to be, but when no one around you is "lost", who do you stay sharp for? Who are you trying to impact?

After living in Texas most of our lives, we were thrust into moving often for work and lived back and forth, from coast to coast, so New England was quite a culture shock! Our first question, to a new acquaintance, in Texas, was, "What church do you go to?" We had no idea how to talk to people where the percentage of Christians was 4% of a state! It was like being on another planet. What we saw over those years was a deep need, not for church goers or fish emblems on more cars, not for more Christian radio stations or cooler worship settings. We needed the one thing we couldn't get without pure, sacrificial, clean hearts that were after God's heart.

What we needed was L O V E!

It was what the world needed too! We didn't even know what that truly looked like before that night in the ER and the few weeks after. People that loved you from the first moment they met you. People that would continue to love you, no matter what issues you had. People that would seek the Lord about how they could bless you and show you a sliver of God's Father heart towards you.

As Pastors Skip and Dee, and those in their little family church, loved us to life, we began to feel a wholeness we had never thought we could feel. We knew all of the right answers. All the Bible verses. All the sermons. But we didn't know the L O V E. We found the Word coming alive like never before. Seeing and experiencing the "perfect L O V E casts out fear" in action. "L O V E covering a multitude of sins" in action in our lives and our marriage. "He binds up the brokenhearted" binding our wounds we thought were healed (but certainly weren't). "The Truth will set you free" functioning through His L O V E, to cancel lies we had thought about ourselves, the church and God himself.

The first time we met Pastor Skip, ("Coach" is what we call him now), was after our first service at his church in western Massachusetts. Almost immediately, he asked for our phone numbers because he wanted to send us daily thoughts and encouragement from him. Of course, we thought that would be good but we could have never dreamed it would have the profound effect on us that it did. This daily personal thought, straight from the Father through the heart of this servant-hearted pastor transformed us and our thinking. It was a stepping stone to take our daily responsibility as Daughters and Sons of the God of the Universe and translate it into everyday, active life. I had done devotionals through the years, as this book will be for you, and had experienced truth going before me in my day, but this was different. It was vibrant enough to capture the heart of a brand new believer as well as a veteran Christian like me. It had relevant truth that I needed. Sometimes it was just a verse or a one liner to meditate on for the day but all of it was based on a Biblical foundation with the Holy Spirit's fresh breath on it. Through these simple text messages and people's actions of love as well as Biblical life-classes at the church, we were being transformed.

I pray this book finds you in the place of having a hungry heart for more of Him. I pray you find other believers to encourage you and to love like Him. I pray you are transformed into that person for others.

That the world may know, in such a time as this.
You are His Champion of LOVE!

Renee Story,
Friend and member of Life Church
Hampden, MA

(This publication was created as a surprise gift for "Coach" to celebrate the 25th anniversary of this church - celebrated November 14th, 2015 - from his church family to honor him for his selfless example of Jesus in our lives... from digging people out from feet of snow to fixing a single widows car, from freshly painting someone's bedroom to simple encouragement phone calls all day long. Thank you for helping mold us all into CHAMPIONS.)

January 1

Champion,

IT'S TIME EVERYONE! It's time to step out, step up, and step into a greater sobriety of who Jesus is and how much the Father loves you. It's time to make Him the highest priority of your life like never before. It's time to come out of intentions and into follow through with what you already know to do. It's time to come out of denial into determination and dedication to the heart of the Father who loves you more than anyone else. It's time to say to hell, NO, and to heaven, YES!!! NO to foolishness and YES to wisdom. THEN, I can guarantee you a Happy New Year, aligned with Heaven's Heart, experiencing the Greatness of God! You will be found overcoming, not overwhelmed; rejoicing, not resenting or regretting; and conquering instead of complaining. Come on Champion! It's Time to stand up and be counted! BE NOT AFRAID, GOD IS WITH YOU!

Joshua 1:9 "This is my command-be strong and courageous! Do not be afraid or discouraged, for the Lord your God is with you WHEREVER YOU GO!"

Champion,

The Lord says "When your heart is SET ON ME and not someone, something, sometime, or some event, then you will be solid, stable, peaceful, and joyful, whether or not that someone, something, or sometime comes to pass! You will be unmovable, unshakable, like a solid rock no matter what, just like Me, says the Lord." You will also be a source of joy, love, peace, wisdom and power to those around you, and that's when life is exciting!

1 Corinthians 15:58 "So my dear brothers and sisters, be strong and immovable. Always work enthusiastically for the Lord, for you know that nothing you do for the Lord is ever useless."

Champion,

Provision is NOT A PROBLEM for a Christian that is seeking first the Kingdom of God and His righteousness! According to Matthew 6:33, He will give you everything you need! God promises that He will meet ALL your needs, (spiritual, emotional, physical, relational and financial), according to His riches in glory. He promises that He will give His kids the desires of their heart! He is a Father that goes beyond more than we could think, ask, or even imagine! So instead of worrying, wondering, or putting your hope or confidence in your job or something other than God's promises and integrity, ask Him to help you, to train you, and show you how to seek first His Kingdom and His righteousness. When you seek Him first, He does great things in your life as you listen and follow. When outside circumstances are trying to tell you something different, RUN to the throne room of Grace with the scriptural promises. The Father is looking for BOLD faith. He is looking for sons and daughters of God that believe, stand, and declare what their Father has said, even in the midst of the opposing circumstances.

Matthew 6:33 "Seek the kingdom of God above all else, and live righteously, and He will give you everything you need."

Champion,

Provision is Not a Problem with God! He says you have been preordained to do good works. To do good works, you need resources, so that means the resources have already been made available, just ask, believe and start thanking Him for all the good resources to do His good works!

Ephesians 2:10 "For we are God's own handiwork His workmanship, recreated in Christ Jesus, born anew that we may do those good works which God predestined planned beforehand for us taking paths which He prepared ahead of time, that we should walk in them living the good life which He prearranged and made ready for us to live."

Champion,

Provision is not a problem for God! Job 22:22-30 Listen to His instructions, and store them in your heart. If you return to the Almighty, you will be restored, so clean up your life. If you give up your lust for money, and throw your precious gold into the river, the Almighty Himself will be your treasure. He will be your precious silver! Then you will take delight in the Almighty and look up to God. You will pray to Him, and He will hear you, and you will fulfill your vows to Him. You will succeed in whatever you choose to do, and light will shine on the road ahead of you. If people are in trouble and you say "Help them," God will save them. Even sinners will be rescued; they will be rescued because your hands are pure.

Job 22:22-30 "Listen to His instructions, and store them in your heart. If you return to the Almighty, you will be restored—so clean up your life."

Champion,

WIN WIN!!! That's what life is like as a Child of God! It's abundant as a follower of Christ. No matter if good or bad things are happening, if you stay in faith, believing, and declaring the truth, you will see that your God is the Way maker, redeemer, restorer, and vindicator. He means what He says and He has the ability to bring it to pass! So if something good happens, thank God! If something bad happens, thank God! You can live unafraid and fully alive, and fully functioning when you realize these truths.

Romans 8:28 "And we know that God causes all things to work together for the good of those who love God and are called according to His purpose for them."

Champion,

Good news for everyone! All the wisdom, understanding, knowledge, and insight you need is available! ALL you need is available. LOOK up, do not GIVE up, because someone is looking out for YOU! Believe and exercise your faith and declare! If you need wisdom, ask our generous God and He will give it to you, He will not rebuke you for asking! So I ask You, Heavenly Father, for all the wisdom that I need, and I thank You for clarity, insight and knowledge to fulfill the good plan that you have for me in JESUS name, amen!

James 1:5 "If you need wisdom, ask our generous God, and will give it to you. He will not rebuke you for asking."

Champion,

If you let any evil thoughts come into your heart, UNCON-TESTED, you will suffer because of it! That's why God tells us to cast down EVERY evil imagination! Ask Him to help you recognize what is evil so that you may not think is innocent will be able to get rid of it immediately. EVERY thought is a seed that has the power to reproduce something in you and through you.

1 Corinthians 10:5 "We destroy (cast down) every proud obstacle that keeps people from knowing God. We capture their rebellious thoughts and teach them to obey Christ."

Champion,

My friend, fellow believer, disciple of Christ, fully manifesting child of God, all this is who He is making you! Within you, you have the power and the authority to make a lot out of little, just like Jesus did! He fed the thousands with a little bread and fish, with the authority and the power His Father gave Him, and you have that same authority and power. STOP USING IT INCORRECTLY! Stop making molehills into mountains. REPENT, and be restored into unity with God and others. Stop complaining, whining, and making excuses, stop feeding your hurt and anger, STOP! You have the authority and power to make things better. STOP using it to make things worse. STOP being miserable and mean when you are hurt and angry! Be like JESUS and make things better. YOU have the power to make a it good day through praise, prayer and prophesying! Choose to speak life!

Proverbs 18:21 "The tongue can bring death or life, those who love to talk will reap the consequences."

Champion,

Good News Everyone! You get to choose! Deuteronomy 30:19 says choose life, and the Apostle Paul focused on doing the profitable thing. YOU get to choose the channel that you listen to and the words YOU LET into your heart! You choose to be afraid or not, and you choose to be angry or not! Listen to channel 777 because it's the one from heaven and it will empower you constantly, strengthen you supernaturally, and even cause health to your body and clarity to your mind! Download it into your heart daily and you can play it wherever you are so you can be free and stay free!

Deuteronomy 30:19 "Today I have given you the choice between life and death, between blessings and curses. Now I call on heaven and earth to witness the choice you make. Oh, that you would choose life, so that you and your descendants might live!"

Champion,

The words you think upon fill your heart and come out your mouth. They either build you up or tear you down, wound you and wear you out, or heal you and energize you. They will lift you up or push you down! If it's the voice of God, then the words are beneficial, if it's the devil's voice, then it is distracting and destructive. BE AWARE and know that you have the power to say NO to the thoughts that are destroying, separating and disconnecting you, and YES to the thoughts that are strengthening you and uniting you to God and others who love you! STOP letting the devil bully you! Stop the victimization and the self-sabotage. You are NOT a victim. You ARE a victor through Jesus Christ and by His strength and you are well able to do this!

1 Corinthians 15:57 "But Thank God! He gives us victory over sin and death through our Lord Jesus Christ!"

Champion,

Fresh food from heaven! Your body needs it and your heart needs it. God's word says man cannot live on bread alone but only can experience abundant life by hearing the voice of God! Come, come, come! All are welcome! You will be overwhelmed with Gods goodness today!

Matthew 4:4 "But Jesus told him "NO! The scriptures say, People do not live by bread alone, but by every word that comes from the mouth of God."

January 13

Champion,

Today there is Fresh Bread of Life! I have heard it said, "Where there is a will, there is a way." Good news!!! God has a will, a perfect will, a good plan for you and He has all the resources to make a way for His good plan to come to pass in your life. So celebrate, because faith celebrates ahead of time. Faith is trusting the truth of who God is before we see something in the natural. Walk by faith, not by sight and don't quit! Faith in our Heavenly Father, and patience, (waiting with cheerful expectations), produces great results! Focus on what God has already done, even if you have to go all the way back to the cross. He always produces what He has promised!

Jeremiah 29:11 "For I know the plans I have for you," says the Lord. "They are plans for good and not for disaster, to give you a future and a hope."

January 14

Champion,

What you value the most you make a priority. Your priorities become habits and habits produce a lifestyle. Your lifestyle produces your future, earthly and eternal. Ask your Heavenly Father to help you value, prioritize, and live the lifestyle that produces a good future, the good plan that He has for you that leaves a legacy that you know would help others! The results are amazing!

Psalms 145:4 "Let each generation tell its children of Your mighty acts; let them proclaim Your power."

Champion,

Here is today's inspiration and declaration: Jesus said this to his people and He is still saying it today. So you can declare: I have the peace of Jesus Christ and my heart is not troubled and I am not afraid! I renounce the spirit of fear from controlling me and I declare the only spirit that controls me is the Holy Spirit of power, love and a sound mind that comes from above, straight from the heart of God.

John 14:27 "Peace I leave with you; my peace I give you. I do not give to you as the world gives. Do not let your hearts be troubled and do not be afraid."

Champion,

My friends, Every time a problem knocks on your door you can either drop to your knees in worry and panic, be offended and disconnected, OR you can drop to your knees to worship and remember WHO YOUR GOD IS !!! Within God's Word are promises that will solve every problem and the One who made those promises has the greatest integrity and ability of all! He doesn't make excuses. My friends, exercise your faith and patience and inquire of what has been made available for you. If you don't know the promises are, then searching them out should be your highest priority. Otherwise you will never live in the full-time peace that passes understanding, and you will never know joy indescribable! So much has been made available to you!

Philippians 4:6 "Then you will experience God's peace, which exceeds anything we can understand. His peace will guard your hearts and minds as you live in Christ Jesus."

Champion,

My friends, come, come, the voice of the One that loves you more than anyone else is calling you to come.

Revelation 22:17 "The Spirit and the bride say "Come." Let anyone who hears this say, "Come." Let anyone who is thirsty come. Let anyone who desires drink freely from the water of life!"

Champion,

No matter what, as a Christian you can expect blessing because Proverbs 22:4 says "True humility and fear of the Lord lead to riches, honor, and long life" So expect honor and abundant life as long as you stay in the place of humility and reverence, for that is when you can expect a blessing. Do not be moved out of that lifestyle because of a circumstance. Do not listen to a lying spirit, do not listen to the spirit of fear, but draw near to the Heart of God and hear His words of encouragement! Stay true and live a full time, daily pattern of humility and reverence for Him. As always, ask Him to help you because you won't be able to do it without His help. The results will be amazing!

PS. If you have fallen away, don't sway anymore, just get up and run back to open arms and the heart of love waiting for you.

Philippians 4:13 "For I can do everything through Christ, who gives me strength."

Champion,

Don't worry, just worship! You either live in worship, honoring God, which produces life, or live in worry, which produces death. You either live a lifestyle of worship, which is faith in action, doing what honors the Father, or you will live a lifestyle of worry, which is another form of worship when you are bowing down to fear and unbelief. This is doing what dishonors the Father. ALWAYS worship no matter what the circumstance looks like! Honor the Father today... the results are amazing.

worry is bowing down to fear!

Philippians 4:6 "Don't worry about anything; instead, pray about everything. Tell God what you need, and thanks Him for all He has done."

Champion,

Ecclesiastes 10:1 Dead flies make the oil of the perfumer give off a foul odor; so a little foolishness in one who is esteemed outweighs wisdom and honor. Complaining, Champion, is a little foolishness that creates a foul odor. It is the manifestation of unbelief, (that Our Heavenly Father cannot produce something good out of bad), it is also un-exercised patience and a bad attitude about being inconvenienced. This creates Dead Flies in Our Hearts, and greater loss for us, who have been esteemed as children of God. Ask God to give you a healthy-clean-pure heart, filled with life, wisdom and love, (which is not moved by personal inconveniences or suffering), but rejoices at every turn. This produces a fragrance that attracts the presence of God and changes everything and it keeps us from free from Dead Flies, that cause us to produce a foul odor.

Ephesians 4:29 "Don't use foul or abusive language. Let everything you say be good and helpful, so that your words will be an encouragement to those who hear them."

Champion,

Do not be bewitched or dismayed, your circumstances do not determine your value or your future. God is your maker. You are valuable and God has a perfect plan.

Psalm 43:5 "Why am I discouraged? Why is my heart so sad? I will put my hope in God! I will praise Him again-my Savior and my God!"

Champion,

Good News, the glory of God is in you. The glory of God is on you. The glory of God is for you. The glory of God is in front of you. The glory of God is behind you. The glory of God is all around you. The glory of God is His presence. The glory of God is His power and the glory of God is His wisdom. The glory of God is His faithfulness. The glory of God is His substance and it is for you. Celebrate the glory of God. Celebrate Him, The Father, Jesus and the Holy Spirit.

Psalm 79:9 "Help us, O God of our salvation! Help us for the glory of your name. Save us and forgive our sins for the honor of your name."

Champion,

Do not join the ranks of the complainers. Honor God and you will be exalted, edified, encouraged, empowered and enabled. You are called to love, edify and encourage.

Peter 5:6-7 "So humble yourselves under the mighty power of God, and at the right time he will lift you up in honor. Give all your worries and cares to God, for he cares about you."

Champion,

This is my dream, God's dream for myself... To be a fully manifesting son of God, doing what Jesus did and even greater. Loving God with all that I am and have. Loving others as myself. Imitating God on a nano-second basis and helping others to pursue this dream. So that the Nations are rocked by the goodness of God, saved by His amazing grace, and empowered to fulfill God's dream for them and their family-establishing Heaven on earth. Live with a righteous purpose and let's all do It with greater passion then ever before. Follow me, I will show you how.

Psalm 18:30 "God's way is perfect. All the Lord's promises prove true. He is a shield for all who look to him for protection."

Champion,

Never cash in your confession that God is good. He is never the problem, but always the answer. Do not allow any level of adversity, pain or problem to cause you to go backwards and say that He is not good. Continue to believe, no matter what you see or feel. Declare Romans 8:28, "Something good is going to come out of this situation. I love God and will not stop loving him because of my Heavenly Father's integrity and ability. He turns my darkness into light." I pray these words enable you and empower you to overcome. When following Jesus, there is always light at the end of the tunnel, even in the tunnel, because He is the light.

Romans 8:28 "And we know that God causes everything to work together for the good of those who love God and are called according to his purpose for them."

Champion,

The Lord is faithful to all his promises, and loving toward all He has made. The Lord never abandons anyone who searches for Him. The Lord says, "I will deliver you". The Lord says, "I will never fail you, I will never forsake you, child of God."

Psalm 145:13 "For your kingdom is an everlasting kingdom. You rule throughout all generations. The Lord always keeps his promises; He is gracious in all he does."

Champion,

Kryptonite thinking, paralyzing, strength stealing thoughts stemming from a bad report or disappointment or circumstance, that are still clinging to you? You feel and say things like, "Why bother? It doesn't matter anyway." Pay Attention, you do matter! You can make the difference you are called to make. Your life does matter. Do not quit. Do not give up. Receive the truth that God is a present help in time of need. Cry out! Don't give up! Bring the hurt and anger to Him. If you run to Him you will experience the help you need. Don't be weary. Ask God for the encouragement you need. Ask Him for new inspiration. He understands and will not make fun of you, or criticize. Remember, our Father is the master at turning things around. Run to Him in desperation, not away from Him. He is always where good change begins. You will be strengthened if you wait on Him.

Jeremiah 1:19 "They will fight you, but they will fail. For I am with you, and I will take care of you."

Champion,

Declare and decree Psalm 23 right now. Say it out loud. Speak it over your life. It will set you free and will energize you. The more you do it, the better you will feel. Your words create your world.

Psalm 23

"The Lord is my shepherd. He feeds, guides, and shields me. I will not lack. He makes me lie down in fresh, tender green pastures. He leads me beside the still and restful waters. He refreshes and restores my soul. He leads me in the paths of righteousness, uprightness and right standing with Him. Yes, though I walk through the deep, sunless valley of the shadow of death, I will fear or dread no evil, for the Lord is with me. His presence protects, provides and guides me and it comforts me. The Lord, my Shepherd prepares a table before me in the presence of my enemies. Almighty God anoints my head with oil, blesses me with favor constantly and my brimming cup runs over. I experience supernatural provision. The goodness, mercy, and unfailing love of my Heavenly Father pursues me and overtakes me all the days of my life, and through the length of my days, the house of the Lord and His presence shall be my dwelling place, His presence is my highest priority."

Champion,

Rejoicing is always better than resenting. Rejoicing strengthens, resenting weakens.

1 Chronicles 16:31 "Let the heavens be glad, and the earth rejoice! Tell all the nations, "The Lord reigns!""

Champion,

Like oxygen is to the body, so encouragement is to the soul. When King David suffered his greatest loss and his mighty men wanted to kill him, he encouraged himself in the Lord. The art of encouraging yourself in the Lord causes you to overcome instead of being overcome. Ask God to help you be an expert and you will be found winning instead of losing, excited instead of depressed.

Joshua 1:9 "This is my command—be strong and courageous! Do not be afraid or discouraged. For the Lord your God is with you wherever you go."

Champion,

God says set your mind on me and you will have peace. Focus on the facts of who God is...He is faithful, truthful and able. You will have faith that empowers you to overcome any natural situations. Go out and make it a good day by the power of His spirit.

Psalm 100:5 "For the Lord is good. His unfailing love continues forever, and his faithfulness continues to each generation."

Champion,

Rejoice and declare champion, almighty God is an ever-present help in time of need and He is my God.

Psalm 36:5 "Your unfailing love, O Lord, is as vast as the heavens; your faithfulness reaches beyond the clouds."

FEBRUARY 2

Champion,

Sorry is not enough. The only thing that will make things right and better is true repentance. There is a "fleshly" sorry that causes you and others to remain the same. When we don't want to experience the pain of true humility that takes responsibility for our actions. Then, there is another sorry that takes responsibility, embraces the pain and says, "by the grace of God, I am going to grow in this area." The "fleshly" sorry is for wimps, those that love the lowlife and keep making excuses to stay there. The Godly sorry creates Champions. Rise up and take responsibility for yourself.

Joel 2:12 [A Call to Repentance] "That is why the Lord says, "Turn to me now, while there is time. Give me your hearts. Come with fasting, weeping, and mourning."

Champion,

The reality of God you meditate on, produces fruit of peace and power. For every hour your thoughts are on what is praiseworthy, excellent and virtuous, His faithfulness, His truthfulness, His ability...He will be with your daily duties and realities. Then you will have wisdom, hope, peace, power and will overcome. Ask Him to help you put all your hope in Him.

Psalm 48:9 "O God, we meditate on your unfailing love as we worship in your Temple."

Champion,

When failure or the fear of suffering intimidates you, the spirit of fear will control you. The spirit of fear drives you, but the Holy Spirit guides you. There will always be peace and joy when you're being guided by the Holy Spirit. There will always be torment when you're being driven by the spirit of fear. Make this declaration, "God Almighty has not given me the spirit of fear, but a spirit of power, love and wisdom."

2 Timothy 1:7 "For God did not give us a spirit of timidity or cowardice or fear, but [He has given us a spirit] of power and of love and of sound judgment and personal discipline [abilities that result in a calm, well-balanced mind and self-control]". (AMP)

Champion,

If you want to fulfill your God-given potential, you must be great at receiving instruction and correction. Even seek it out. If you do, there will be many rewards.

Proverbs 13:18 "If you ignore criticism, you will end in poverty and disgrace; if you accept correction, you will be honored."

FEBRUARY 6

Champion,

Wisdom is sensitivity to the Holy Spirit. He will show you what to do, when, where and how. It is only by the leadership and power of the Holy Spirit that you will overcome and move mountains instead of being moved by them. It is only by the leadership and power of the Holy Spirit that you will fulfill your destiny, and hear at the end of your time (Luke19: 17) ."Well done thou good and faithful servant".

Proverbs 4:5-15 "Get skillful and godly Wisdom, get understanding, discernment, comprehension, and interpretation. Do not forget and do not turn back from the words of my mouth."

Champion,

Nurture, it is what every Heart needs. It is what every Heart seeks. It means to cherish, care for and encourage. It is the foundational ingredient needed for the full development of every person. Every person is like a tree that needs the rain of cherishing, the sunshine of care and the refreshing air of encouragement. The Heavenly Father is a nurturer, which comes from His perfect love so that we may experience abundant life. He has given us His Word and His Spirit to nurture us. If you draw near, He will draw near and nurture you and give you what your Heart needs most of All.

Psalm 36:7 "How precious is your unfailing love, O God! All humanity finds shelter in the shadow of your wings."

Champion,

This is what God is saying every moment of every day because it is the foundation of everything else He wants you to know; My Friends, God is Love and His love is kind, patient, everlasting, unconditional, forgiving, perfect, pure and powerful. It never fails. It covers a multitude of sin, heals, comforts, encourages, lifts up, builds up, leads, teaches and helps people experience new freedom. It is the greatest of all. Faith, hope and love, because it is the catalyst, the beginning point, the main ingredient of every recipe of God's goodness. It is your greatest need. Ask Him for fresh love, spend time recognizing you are beloved-deeply, dearly valued and cared for. Spend time thanking Him for that, it will heal you, set you free and strengthen you.

Romans 8:38 "And I am convinced that nothing can ever separate us from God's love. Neither death nor life, neither angels nor demons, neither our fears for today nor our worries about tomorrow—not even the powers of hell can separate us from God's love."

Champion,

Who you are is more important than what you do. If what you do is not done with love, kindness and patience, the Lord says it's just a bunch of noise, but has no reward. (1 Cor. 13) Who you are, a person of quality character, love, joy, peace, goodness. Patient, kind, manifesting self control and faithful walking in humility and reverence for Almighty God-operating according to the wisdom of God. These things need to be our highest priority. You are like a tree and these are the fruits that you can manifest. Your heart is like a field and the Father, by His Spirit is the farmer. If you yield to the leadership of His Spirit, He will help you keep your heart watered with the word of God and bathed in the sunshine of His presence. Embrace the process and you will be very glad that you did. You will go from peace to peace and strength to strength and experience much victory and overcome in ways that you never have before.

1 Peter 2:9 "But you are not like that, for you are a chosen people. You are royal priests, a holy nation, God's very own possession. As a result, you can show others the goodness of God, for he called you out of the darkness into his wonderful light."

Champion,

God is not looking to rearrange, but to change. Let go so He can lift you up and out of the old into the new. You can trust Him. No one loves you more. Don't try to figure it out--He already has. Just give it all to Him. He is the master craftsman and what He makes is very good. Give Him your heart, give Him your hands, give Him your life and He will make something beautiful out of it and do great exploits with it. Nothing will satisfy you more.

2 Corinthians 5:17 "This means that anyone who belongs to Christ has become a new person. The old life is gone; a new life has begun!"

My Friend,

Jesus, Jesus, Jesus . . . beautiful, amazing Jesus. Son of God, faithful and strong, wise, amazing Jesus. He is talented, well-spoken, always-available-- Jesus. Jesus is caring, sharing and always ready to lift you up and help you out. The one that made a way for you, that became the door to experience heaven's goodness now and forever. The one that has never forsaken, forgotten, abandoned, rejected or betrayed you. Jesus loves you, wants you, values you and paid the price for you to be forgiven and set free, delivered and healed—if you ask. No one and nothing else deserves your heart, your worship, more than Him. Put all your hope in Him. The results are amazing.

Psalm 37:27-28 "Turn from evil and do good, and you will live in the land forever. For the LORD loves justice, and he will never abandon the godly."

Champion,

Someone's behavior can be wrong and irritate you and you can respond in anger. Or, someone's behavior can be wrong and you can respond in compassion. The difference between an angry response and a compassionate response, (both designed to produce a better behavior), is usually consists of a few things. First, it identifies the condition of our heart and how much true love we have for people. 1 Peter 4:8 Above all things have intense and unfailing love for one another, for love covers a multitude of sins, forgives and disregards the offenses of others. It can also identify whether we're living with a passion to benefit others or a passion to benefit ourselves. Ask God to help you adjust your priorities, values and motives to where your highest goal is to benefit others. That is the true heart of Jesus and that is what He did and continues to do every day.

1 Peter 4:8 "Above all things have intense and unfailing love for one another, for love covers a multitude of sins, forgives and disregards the offenses of others."

Champion,

Jesus said we could worship mammon (money) or Him in Matthew 6:24. Giving your heart to mammon will cause subtraction and division even when it promises addition and multiplication. Giving your heart to Jesus and following His principles will lead to addition and multiplication. If it doesn't seem that way-stay faithful, because that is what brings Him pleasure and He deserves that for what He has already done.

Matthew 6:24 "No one can serve two masters. For you will hate one and love the other; you will be devoted to one and despise the other. You cannot serve both God and money."

Champion,

Proverbs 14:30 says that a calm and undisturbed mind and heart are the life and health of the body, but envy, jealousy, and wrath are like rottenness of the bones. Jealousy is a form of complaining. "I don't have what they have. I don't have what I want right now and they do." It's the trap of comparison that destroys peace. It's the spirit of death coming against you. Resist immediately! Do not cooperate with it! It stems from a lack of knowledge, or rejecting knowledge that God has a good plan for you. Let patience do a perfect work and persevere.

Proverbs 14:30 "A peaceful heart leads to a healthy body; jealousy is like cancer in the bones."

Champion,

You will reap whatever good plan God has for you. Do not give up on God! Remember, jealousy can be a form of unbelief when faith in God's faithfulness, integrity and ability is not being stirred up through rejoicing for the other person. Do not let it in. It will destroy you. Get rid of it quickly. Ask God for complete deliverance and the help to keep it out. By the way you already have the best thing if you have said yes to Jesus--His presence! Prioritize that, seek that. It's the source of all that you truly need.

Psalm 71:14 "But I will hope continually and will praise You yet more and more." (AMP)

Champion,

Living to benefit the heart of our Heavenly Father and others is the greatest, most rewarding, most fulfilling life. The only thing that will stop you from experiencing it is when the Holy Spirit tells you to do something and you don't do it because you don't want to suffer. What I have found out is if the fear of suffering stops you from following what Jesus is asking you to do, you will cause even greater suffering for yourself and others. I have found out that the fear of suffering keeps us from being in alignment with the Heart of God and saying yes to Jesus. It is the very thing that knocks us out of alignment with His leadership and good plan for our lives and others. Ask God to help you. He is like a great father helping a child learn how to ride a bicycle-patient and kind- but persevering, wanting us to succeed at knowing and flowing with Him. It produces the greatest good.

1 Peter 5:10 "In his kindness God called you to share in his eternal glory by means of Christ Jesus. So after you have suffered a little while, he will restore, support, and strengthen you, and he will place you on a firm foundation."

Champion,

If you are a believer in Christ - saved, born again by the grace of God, putting your faith in the facts, surrendering to the leadership of Jesus and you continue to trust and follow Him--everything is going to work out. And if it looks like it's not- everything is going to work out. Be not afraid! Resist the spirit of fear with the truth and declare, "My God is the Heavenly Father and He turns evil into good. I choose to believe Romans 8:28 that all things work together for good for those that love God, and I will not stop loving God. I will not be seduced into the 'why?' question, but stand up and declare my God is a God of miracles and I will see the goodness of God in the land of the living. My God is a deliverer, Psalm-4:19 He delivers me out of all the evils that confront me, when I put my trust in Him."

Psalm 18:2 "The LORD is my rock, my fortress, and my savior; my God is my rock, in whom I find protection. He is my shield, the power that saves me, and my place of safety."

My Friend,

My friend, because of what Jesus ALREADY DID, you ALWAYS have a reason to praise Him. The Lord says rejoice anyway, and when you do, the enemy will flee seven ways and you will be energized and mobilized by My spirit.

Deuteronomy 28:7 "The LORD will conquer your enemies when they attack you. They will attack you from one direction, but they will scatter from you in seven!"

Champion,

The more revelation of who God is and His promises, the more peace you will have and the more you will be fortified to resist the spirit of fear that causes anger, dread, anxiety, and depression. Fear causes disorder internally and externally, like panic attacks and timidity, which create much loss.

Philippians 4:6-7 "Don't worry about anything; instead, pray about everything. Tell God what you need, and thank him for all he has done. Then you will experience God's peace, which exceeds anything we can understand. His peace will guard your hearts and minds as you live in Christ Jesus."

Champion,

Keep your Hallelujah ON, Champion. It's the garment of praise that will set you free and keep you free. Remember, it's the new song that causes deliverance.

Psalm 32:7 "For you are my hiding place; you protect me from trouble. You surround me with songs of victory."

Champion,

Hardening your heart means you are saying to yourself, "I don't need to pay attention. I don't need to listen. I'm okay. I don't need help." Let go, my friend, lay it down. Avoiding the suffering that you don't want to experience if you yield to the Holy Spirit and what He is saying to you is going to cause greater suffering.

Proverbs 28:13-14, "He who covers his transgressions will not prosper, but whoever confesses and forsakes his sins will obtain mercy. Blessed happy, fortunate, and to be envied is the man who reverently and worshipfully fears the Lord at all times regardless of circumstances, but he who hardens his heart will fall into calamity." (AMP)

Champion,

Somebody loves you more than anyone else and has done more for you than anybody else. Follow His voice today. It leads to abundant life.

Romans 8:32 "Since he did not spare even his own Son but gave him up for us all, won't he also give us everything else?"

Champion,

You have a strategy for a strong, stable, victorious, overcoming life that honors God and produces great results and great rewards. For He is a Rewarder of those that diligently seek Him- Hebrews-11:6b.

Matthew 7:24-27 "So everyone who hears these words of Mine and acts upon them, obeying them, will be like a sensible prudent, practical, wise man who built his house upon the rock. And the rain fell and the floods came and the winds blew and beat against that house; yet it did not fall, because it had been founded on the rock. And everyone who hears these words of Mine and does not do them -will be like a stupid, foolish man who built his house upon the sand. And the rain fell and the floods came and the winds blew and beat against that house, and it fell—and great and complete was the fall of it." (AMP)

FEBRUARY 24

Champion,

Motives matter, Champion. Are you aware of yours? It's very important. Both John the Baptist and Jesus rebuked certain people, identifying the spirit working through them, calling them serpents and vipers, (Matt.3:7&23:33), and wicked and lazy (25:26). Ask God to help you be aligned with His heart with pure, unselfish motives, trusting Him that He will make a way for His good plan to come to pass in your life. Because usually it's fear that you are going to miss out on something you want that causes you to operate, manipulate and dominate with impure motives. It happens many times in very subtle ways, seen by God even if they are not seen by others. Let's ask for forgiveness when we recognize what's really going on inside of us. It will be granted. Aim for the voice of God saying, "Well done, thou good and faithful servant."

1 Samuel 16:7b ". . .The LORD doesn't see things the way you see them. People judge by outward appearance, but the LORD looks at the heart."

Champion,

Your diet and exercise program makes a big difference, but that alone is not enough. Wisdom says ask the greatest teacher, the Holy Spirit, to give you the words of life that the Father has for you today.

Matthew 4:4 "People do not live on bread alone, but on every word that comes from the mouth of God."

Champion,

Jesus lived a surrendered life. He was convinced of his Father's love for Him, allowing Him the freedom to pursue and fulfill his destiny. He left a lasting legacy...the world would never be the same because of this quest. Inconvenience, pain and even coming face to face with death did not stop Him. We are called to do the same. Let's follow in the footsteps of the greatest One who has ever lived.

Revelation 12:11 "And they defeated him by the blood of the Lamb and by their testimony. And they did not love their lives so much that they were afraid to die."

Champion,

When you are hurt and angry, do not lash out. Find a private place and cry out to the Father. He will heal your hurting heart. Take your hurt and anger to Him immediately and stay there until peace replaces pain...

Revelation 21:4 "He will wipe away every tear from their eyes, and there will be no more death or sorrow or crying or pain. All these things are gone forever."

Champion,

The words you speak produce life or death. Words are seeds that create. Your heart is the seed container. What you meditate on drops down as a seed into your heart and comes out of your mouth, determining your future...

Luke 8:15 "And the seeds that fell on the good soil represent honest, good-hearted people who hear God's word, cling to it, and patiently produce a huge harvest."

Champion,

Rejection will cause pain. When that pain is left unattended, it causes deterioration of our soul and the weightiness of sorrow can break our spirit. Your enemy, the devil, uses people to spread hurt. Choose to forgive and pray for the person who hurt you. Jesus will meet you in that place and take every ounce of pain away. It's time to let it go...

Matthew 5:11-12 "God blesses you when people mock you, and persecute you and lie about you, and say all kinds of evil things against you because you are my followers. Be happy about it! Be very glad! For a great reward awaits you in heaven."

Champion,

Some people make excuses, while some people make progress. Ask the Father for new revelation, inspiration and motivation! He will help you overcome by His Spirit. Remember, don't try...Rely on Him. Simply say, "Help me, Jesus...help me, Jesus." He forsakes no one that wholeheartedly seeks Him.

1 Peter 5:7 "Give all your worries and cares to God, for he cares about you."

Champion,

Un-teachableness, lack of humility and lack of reverence for God's wisdom will destroy your life. On the contrary, being teachable, humble and respecting for God's wisdom will create an unstoppable vision for your future...

Proverbs 22:4 "The reward of humility [that is, having a realistic view of one's importance] and the [reverent, worshipful] fear of the Lord Is riches, honor, and life." (AMP)

Champion,

When something is hard, many people quit. Don't quit during the hard times. See them as opportunities to grow up and out of the old. Say, "Hard is good!" Choose life and say out loud, " I can do everything God is showing me to do, by His strength that strengthens me!"

Philippians. 4:13 "For I can do everything through Christ who gives me strength."

anything he gives me to do.

Champion,

Remember, problems are opportunities to learn. Don't accept the virus of disappointment and discouragement. Despair will follow and destroy you. Remember who God is...Remember He is with you...Stir up the gift of truth inside of you and new strength will fill you. *action*

you already have it
greater is he in you

2 Timothy 1:6 "This is why I remind you to fan into flames the spiritual gift God gave you when I laid my hands on you."

7 for God has not given us the spirit of fear, but of love of power and of a sound mind.

Champion,

What is impossible for man is possible for God. All things are possible for those who believe Him. Believing is active. It requires trusting, leaning and adhering. God makes a way where there seems to be no way...Start believing!

God is able to do more than we can imagine or think.

Matt 17:20 mustard seed
Isaiah 41:10 with us
Mark 11:24
Jerm 32:17 nothing too hard
32:27 nothing too hard

Matthew 19:26 "Jesus looked at them intently and said, "Humanly speaking, it is impossible. But with God everything is possible."

Luke 1:37 for with God nothing shall be impossible

Phil 4:13   Mark 10:27
9:23

Champion,

Draw near to Him. Enter His presence. Thank Him for His goodness. Praise Him only and the essence of His presence will cause a refreshing and strengthening. It is invigorating! Take a power shower to start your day!

Psalm 100:4-5 "Enter his gates with thanksgiving; go into his courts with praise. Give thanks to him and praise his name. For the LORD is good. His unfailing love continues forever, and his faithfulness continues to each generation."

Champion,

The condition of your heart is seen through your words and actions. Ask God to change your heart. Like taking a physical shower, enter into a private place and ask Him to cleanse you and fill your heart with new love and wisdom. If you do this, your words and actions will be different. They will become life producing instead of life reducing. It is the best way to live and it changes everything for the better!

Deuteronomy 30:19 "Today I have given you the choice between life and death, between blessings and curses. Now I call on heaven and earth to witness the choice you make. Oh, that you would choose life, so that you and your descendants might live!"

Champion,

King David testified in the book of Psalms that God put gladness in his heart. Ask Him to remove all sadness and madness and establish gladness in your heart today...

Joy that passes understanding

Psalm 4:7 "You have given me greater joy than those who have abundant harvests of grain and new wine."

Champion,

Speaking when you are offended is like adding salt to a wound. It will just create more pain. Take your offense to the Father who is the provider of peace. Talk to Him before you talk to anyone else. He will show you what to do.

Isaiah 26:3 "You will keep in perfect peace all who trust in you, all whose thoughts are fixed on you!"

Champion,

Resenting leads to death and destruction. Rejoicing leading to life and abundance. Ask God to heal your heart and help you rejoice in the midst of suffering...the results are amazing!

Philippians 4:4 "Always be full of joy in the Lord. I say it again--rejoice!"

Champion,

Remember this: Born to bless, live to give, love to serve. Ask the Holy Spirit to help you...it's the best way to live!

Romans 12:11 "Never be lazy, but work hard and serve the Lord enthusiastically."

Champion,

Ask the Heavenly Father to help you live according to the Law of Love, not the love of the law. Live out of the place of life and death, not right and wrong. Then you will have the wisdom to respond, not react.

Law of Love
at all times
to everyone

life death
vs
right/wrong

Romans 12:9-10 *"Don't just pretend to love others. Really love them. Hate what is wrong. Hold tightly to what is good. Love each other with genuine affection and take delight in honoring each other."*

Champion,

Do not let irritations stay in your heart. Ask the Father to help you when you are irritated. Lift it up to Him. He will show you how to pray all the way through until you have a peace in your heart that has replace the irritants. This exercise produces amazing results!

Ephesians 4:26 "And don't sin by letting anger control you. Don't let the sun go down while you are still angry, for anger gives a foothold to the devil."

Champion,

Remember that your "problem" is not the main problem. It is your attitude that either shrinks or expands the problem. If we have been meditating on who God is and His willingness to help, we will be prepared/fortified against the fear and anger that come to wipe us out in the midst of the "problem".

Romans 5:3-5 "We can rejoice, too, when we run into problems and trials, for we know that they help us develop endurance. And endurance develops strength of character, and character strengthens our confident hope of salvation. And this hope will not lead to disappointment. For we know how dearly God loves us, because he has given us the Holy Spirit to fill our hearts with His love."

Champion,

There are 3 things that the physical body needs: quality nutrition, exercise and functioning waste removal through our organs. There are also 3 things our hearts need:

1. Quality nutrition-Spirit and Life supplements (from God's Word),

2. Spiritual exercise: which includes remembering and speaking those words of life back to ourselves,

3. Removal of toxins and waste material: idle words, offenses and irritation.

Follow this regimen and remain healthy inside and out...

1 Timothy 4:8 "Physical training is good, but training for godliness is much better, promising benefits in this life and in the life to come."

Champion,

A lifestyle of praise results in continual refreshing. Remembering who God is by His nature and what He has already done in your life is the catalyst for praise.

Psalm 146:2 "I will praise the LORD as long as I live. I will sing praises to my God with my dying breath."

Champion,

Rejoicing opens the door for new revelation to solve your problem. Resenting and complaining shuts the door and cause greater frustration.

Philippians 2:14 "Do everything without complaining and arguing, 1so that no one can criticize you."

Champion,

Remember, God wants to be your first responder. When the winds of adversity blow in, remember He is bigger, better, wiser. Victory comes from putting <u>all</u> your hope in Him.

Romans 15:13 "I pray that God, the source of hope, will fill you completely with joy and peace because you trust in him. Then you will overflow with confident hope through the power of the Holy Spirit."

Champion,

Everyone enjoys power steering and power brakes on a car. A power-assisted life is available for you through Jesus. Surrender and your heart will remain tender. Listen to His voice that empowers and enables. Let's live for His glory!

Ephesians 3:20 "Now all glory to God, who is able, through his mighty power at work within us, to accomplish infinitely more than we might ask or think."

infinitely more is a lot - so far beyond our thinking

Champion,

A gun not kept cleaned and oiled can backfire and kill you. A car not maintained properly can do the same thing. So it is with our heart...out of the abundance of the heart the mouth speaks, and what the mouth speaks produces life or death. Ask your Heavenly Father for the cleansing and infilling that you need to be a distributor of Life!

Luke 6:45 "A good person produces good things from the treasury of a good heart, and an evil person produces evil things from the treasury of an evil heart. What you say flows from what is in your heart."

Champion,

Do not let the shell of resentment contain you. Resentment makes everything harder. Remember that God is with you, for you, and in you. Rise up mighty champion of God!

Isaiah 40:31 "But those who trust in the LORD will find new strength. They will soar high on wings like eagles. They will run and not grow weary. They will walk and not faint."

Champion,

Compassion is the catalyst for kindness, and the fruit of God's goodness. It has the power to suffocate evil forces such as discouragement and isolation. Ask the Heavenly Father for understanding and the wisdom that causes compassion to rise up in your heart. This life force flowing out of you will destroy works of evil while covering the situation you face with kindness.

Proverbs 3:3 "Never let loyalty and kindness leave you! Tie them around your neck as a reminder. Write them deep within your heart."

Champion,

Good news! All the answers you need are available through your connection with Jesus, by His Word and by His Spirit. You are connected to the mega brain of the universe that knows everything you will ever need to know to succeed in this life and forevermore!

Matthew 14:1 "Do not let your hearts be troubled. You believe in God; believe also in me."

Champion,

Don't live your life based on what other people are doing, but base your life on what Jesus wants to do through you. Ask the Father for the strength and the help to cooperate with Him.

Ephesians 5:1-2 "Imitate God, therefore, in everything you do, because you are his dear children. Live a life filled with love, following the example of Christ. He loved us and offered himself as a sacrifice for us, a pleasing aroma to God."

Champion,

God says to be not afraid or intimidated. He is with you and will strengthen and uphold you with His mighty right hand. Now declare what He has spoken and resurrection power and life that exudes from Him will flow in you and through you. The first work of faith is to speak what God has spoken. Say what He has said and you will be fed and found strong, not weak!

Isaiah 41:10 "Don't be afraid, for I am with you. Don't be discouraged, for I am your God. I will strengthen you and help you. I will hold you up with my victorious right hand."

Champion,

Let's lay down our lives like Jesus did for the benefit of others. Also, be aware of what the Holy Spirit is asking you to fast in preparation for Resurrection Sunday.

Romans 12:1 "And so, dear brothers and sisters, I plead with you to give your bodies to God because of all he has done for you. Let them be a living and holy sacrifice—the kind he will find acceptable. This is truly the way to worship him."

Champion,

This is the season, my friend. This month we celebrate the memory of the Heavenly Father's and Jesus' heroic plan. They are the ones that love you more than anybody else. They said, "yes" to the crucifixion, the most brutal death of all. They said, we will deny ourselves. Jesus said, even if I suffer, I came for the benefit of my Father's good plan. I came to make a way for the benefit of others, so they would have an opportunity to taste and see the goodness of my Father's presence, power, love and wisdom. Let's honor them more every day by drawing near to them by giving our hearts to them more than anybody or anything else. Let's live to please Him, by the power He gives us when we draw near and live to benefit others, everywhere we are, at all times. Then you will experience a truly abundant life and hear Him say to you, "Well done."

James 4:8 "Come close to God, and God will come close to you. Wash your hands, you sinners; purify your hearts, for your loyalty is divided between God and the world."

Champion,

Practice spirit and soul diligence, my friend. Practice eating and drinking the bread of life and the living water, rejoicing instead of complaining, rejoicing instead of resenting because you remember the word of God says that all things work together for good for those that love Him and are called according to his purpose (Romans 8:28). Practice exercising your faith based on the integrity and the faithfulness of God instead of being controlled by fear of suffering. All of the above determines whether you are influencing people with life or death. Let's live to bless others by maintaining internal health so encouragement and edification comes out of our mouth.

Luke 6:45 "A good person produces good things from the treasury of a good heart, and an evil person produces evil things from the treasury of an evil heart. What you say flows from what is in your heart."

Champion,

Rejoicing causes victory and complaining causes death. Rejoicing causes victory and then victory causes more rejoicing! That is called the supernatural life cycle, the supernatural slinky principal. Philippians 4:4 Rejoice in the Lord always delight, gladden yourselves in Him; again I say, Rejoice! Why you say? Because, if your gladness comes from anything else other than who He is and what He has already done, your joy can be stolen. Do the spirit strategy, not the flesh strategy, and you will overcome instead of being overcome.

Philippians 4:4 "Always be full of joy in the Lord. I say it again—rejoice!"

sing rejoice in the lord always and again I pay rejoice He love is everywhere-

Champion,

When you focus on what you've already been given, which is a covenant with God, and the fact that all that is His is available to you and provision is not a problem, instead of what you're not getting when you want it, (which is the source that causes complaining), you will be a consistent rejoicer. You will be delivered from the poison of impatience, hurt, anger, resentment, jealousy and much more. Operate by His wisdom and you will see amazing results that honor Him. That should be our greatest priority.

Genesis 22:14 "Abraham named the place Yahweh-Yireh (which means "the LORD will provide"). To this day, people still use that name as a proverb: "On the mountain of the LORD it will be provided."

Champion,

When people don't do what you want them to do, ask God to help you not be mad, offended and/or judgmental. Don't say I don't care, say my Heavenly Father provides for me and He will make away for me to know the goodness He has for me.

Control is in control
love at all times

Isaiah 43:19 "For I am about to do something new. See, I have already begun! Do you not see it? I will make a pathway through the wilderness. I will create rivers in the dry waste-land."

SELAH

Take a few moments to reflect on the past three months and evaluate how this has effected your daily life. Pray and ask the Lord to highlight what you need to remember. Record your thoughts here...

We are more than we think

We have everything in him

We are loved

Champion,

Cancer of the soul is more dangerous than cancer of the body because cancer of the body can kill one person. Cancer of the soul can kill so many more. Cancer of the soul keeps the fruit of the Spirit from manifesting, which is love, joy, peace goodness, kindness, patience, faith, humility and self-control, which are the most powerful forces. From my understanding, cancer of the body is the fruit of independent destructive cells devouring instead of empowering. So it is with cancer of the soul. Cancer of the soul is independent, unchecked thoughts, devouring instead of empowering.

Galatians 5:22-23 "But the Holy Spirit produces this kind of fruit in our lives: love, joy, peace, patience, kindness, goodness, faithfulness, gentleness, and self-control. There is no law against these things!"

Champion,

Scripture talks about renewing the mind with the wisdom of God and casting down evil imaginations, and casting your cares on the one who loves you more than anyone else and has the power and willingness to help you. That's why God wrote the Bible, because He knows the power of right thinking and wrong thinking. Ask Him to help you to think higher thoughts that empower instead of devour you and others.

Romans 12:2 "Don't copy the behavior and customs of this world, but let God transform you into a new person by changing the way you think. Then you will learn to know God's will for you, which is good and pleasing and perfect."

Champion,

The smartest thing anyone could ever do is to give their heart to the Father, Son and Holy Spirit, and trust them on a nanosecond basis. Ask Him to help you be idolatry-free, constantly putting your hope in Him, going to Him first when you are in need. Let Him be your first source of comfort and help, getting your foundational value, acceptance and love from Him. There is no other way to live a life of peace and joy, unmoved by the behavior of others or the circumstances of life.

Psalm 62:5 "Let all that I am wait quietly before God, for my hope is in him."

Champion,

Some people say that attitude is everything. I would say it exposes everything that is going on inside of a person, manifesting in either words or behavior. Attitude is the fruit of a person's thinking and reveals the health of a person's heart. So the greatest priority is recognizing what you are thinking and why. Attitude is the fruit of the thoughts that you are receiving and thinking upon. Attitude is the fruit of your interpretation of what's going on. Attitude is the fruit of what's going on internally and how you are handling what's going on internally. It is the mirror of what you are doing with the thoughts that are bombarding you. Attitude is fruit. It's neither the problem nor the answer. The root unseen is the source of the good or bad attitude. You can't change attitude or improve it until your heart is healed and filled with accurate thinking.

Philippians 4:8 "And now, dear brothers and sisters, one final thing. Fix your thoughts on what is true, and honorable, and right, and pure, and lovely and admirable. Think about things that are excellent and worth of praise."

Champion,

One of the ways you grow up and mature and become the Champion through Jesus, that you have the potential to become is a willingness, even a hunger for wisdom and instruction, knowledge and correction. All of these are gifts from God, but the most powerful and helpful gift can be correction. But for many, correction has a negative context because of past events that leave people feeling like failures. So, correction to them reinforces what they feel about themselves. And the gift of correction is not received, not pursued. The humility that opens the door for correction does not manifest because we are so defensive, not wanting to feel the pain. But, the pain is not as much about the healthy correction available that could help us. But, the unhealed wounds from negative correction of the past. The Lord says that the gift of correction is an act of love and an act of being honored. It is designed to empower you, set you in alignment with God's good plan for you. So ask God to help you receive the gift of healthy correction. And not be defensive, keeping yourself trapped and lacking, perishing, instead of moving forward and prospering.

Proverbs 3:11-12 "My child, don't reject the Lord's discipline, and don't be upset when He corrects you. For the Lord corrects those He loves, just as a father corrects a child in whom he delights."

Champion,

What you value, becomes a part of your life. You draw near to it and it draws near to you. What you value the most is what you rely on the most. It's your priority, it's what you must have and can't live without. It controls you, it is your God. What is your God? Who is your God? Do you even have the courage to be honest? Please!! Choose life today, every day. Make the one that loves you more than anyone else your highest priority! Love Him back today and every day. John 14:6 Jesus said "I am the way the truth and the life, no one experiences the goodness of God my Father without my leadership". Revere and draw near and He will steer you into true abundant life.

John 14:6 "Jesus told him,"I am the way, the truth, and the life. No one can come to the Father except through Me."

Champion,

There is a worldly way to live and a Godly way to live. Jesus said choose life. If you love me, do what I have taught you to do. Do what you know in your heart I am telling you to do. Love for Jesus, from the revelation that He loves us more than anybody else, empowers us to trust Him; to let go of the old and walk into the new, the unknown. It's the bully called fear of suffering that keeps us pretending everything is okay, instead of following in the way. Ask Him to help you follow.

John 10:27 "My sheep listen to my voice; I know them, and they follow me."

My Friends,

Plumbing problems require a plumber, electrical problems require an electrician etc. Many times problems get worse when you rely on someone that does not know what they're doing, or does not have the expertise needed. So it is with people problems. Go to a people mechanic - a relationship specialist, someone that understands the inner workings of the soul and heart. You must recognize, am I talking of someone who can contain the virus? And are they going to help heal my heart and stop the virus? You must identify the motive of your heart for why you are spewing. Is it for breakthrough because you know the person you're talking to can help you overcome? Or are you just looking for sympathy, looking for people to agree with you of how bad you have it? When you are hurt and angry, do not spread the poison in your heart. Like any other problem, find an expert that can help you.

Proverbs 3:5-6 "Trust in the Lord with all your heart; do not depend on your own understanding. Seek His will in all you do, and He will show you which path to take."

Champion,

Promise Food

Psalm 37:3-5, 8 --Trust lean on, rely on, and be confident in the Lord and do good; so shall you dwell in the land and feed surely on His faithfulness, and truly you shall be fed. Delight yourself also in the Lord, and He will give you the desires and secret petitions of your heart. Commit your way to the Lord roll and repose each care of your load on Him; trust lean on, rely on, and be confident also in Him and He will bring it to pass. Cease from anger and forsake wrath; fret not yourself—it tends only to evildoing.

Psalm 37:3-5,8 "Trust in the Lord and do goo. Then you will live safely in the land and prosper. Take delight in the Lord, and He will give you your heart desires. Commit everything you do to the Lord, Trust Him, and He will help you. Stop being angry! Turn from your rage! Do not lose your temper- it only leads to harm."

Champion,

Psalm 103:1-5, 8 Bless affectionately, gratefully praise the Lord, O my soul; and all that is <u>deepest within me, bless</u> His holy name! Bless affectionately, gratefully praise the Lord, O my soul, and FORGET not one of all His benefits. Who forgives every one of all your iniquities? <u>Who heals each one</u> of all your diseases? Who redeems your life from the pit and corruption? Who beautifies, dignifies, and crowns you with loving-kindness and tender mercy? Who satisfies your mouth, your necessity and desire at your personal age and situation with good so that your youth, renewed, is like the eagle's, strong, overcoming, soaring? The Lord is merciful and gracious, slow to anger and plenteous in mercy and loving-kindness.

Psalm 103:1-5,8 "Let all that I am praise the Lord; with my whole heart, I will praise His holy name. Let all that I am praise the lord; may I never forget the good things He does for me. He forgives all my sins and heals all my diseases. He redeems me form death and crowns me with love and tender mercies. He fills my life with good things. My youth is renewed like the eagle's. The Lord is compassionate and merciful, slow to get angry and filled with unfailing love."

Champion,

Here is the strategy that leads to true success! Proverbs 16:1-3 The plans of the mind and orderly thinking belong to man, but from the Lord comes the wise answer of the tongue. All the ways of a man are pure in his own eyes, but the Lord weighs the spirits, the thoughts and intents of the heart. Roll your works upon the Lord. Commit and trust them wholly to Him; He will cause your thoughts to become agreeable to His will, and so shall your plans be established and succeed.

Proverbs 16:1-3 "We can make our own plans, but the Lord gives the right answer. People may be pure in their own eyes but the Lord examines their motives. Commit your actions to the Lord, and your plans will succeed."

Champion,

The Lord says that your anger cannot produce what My Spirit can. He says do not lash out but look up. Bring your hurting heart, all the frustration, and anger to Him. And He will transform your pain into peace and then you will know pleasure from the power of His presence. There is no other Comforter that can heal you. Your heart will never be healed or made whole with a microwave; it needs the oven of God's presence, His touch, and His wisdom. You will never experience the peace that passes understanding by the quick fix of yelling, quarreling, retreating, drugs, cigarettes, sex, alcohol, food, vacation, success, money, fitness, praise, acceptance of people or any other subtle, seducing false god. The Father in Heaven who created you, the one that has a good plan for you, must be your consistent constant hope. You will be consistently derailed and offended and in the constant torment of regret. Ask God to help you be idolatry free. Delivered from investing your hope in the wrong thing, so that even the blessings He has given you, won't be your foundational source of peace and joy, only Him.

John 14:27 "I am leaving you with a gift—peace of mind and heart. And the peace I give is a gift the world cannot give. So don't be troubled or afraid."

Champion,

Good News! Almighty God, Our Heavenly Father, is the Rewarder. Hebrews 11:5-6 Because of faith, Enoch was caught up and transferred to heaven, so that he did not have a glimpse of death; and he was not found, because God had translated him. For even before he was taken to heaven, he received testimony, (still on record), that he had pleased and been satisfactory to God. But without faith, (trusting, following, yielding to Him), it is impossible to please and be satisfactory to Him. For whoever would come near to God must necessarily believe that God exists and that He is the Rewarder of those who earnestly and diligently seek Him out. Invest your hope; trust your heart to the one that deserves it more than anyone else. It will pay the greatest dividends.

John 14:1 "Don't let your hearts be troubled. Trust in God, and trust also in me."

My Friend,

Jeremiah 2:13 says "God is the Fountain of Living Water." Drink up!! Nothing else will satisfy. The more you do, the more you will recognize the value and it will become a priority, then a habit and you will overcome like you never have before. You will walk in the strength and the power of God, fear will not steer you. Courage that conquers and wisdom that wins will flow out of you. Please hear the Heart of God. Put all your hope in Him. There are many fountains that promise, but only one that produces, profits and causes true prosperity in every area of your life. Massive freedom awaits you and those you love.

Psalms 36:9 "For You are the fountain of life, the Light by which we see."

April 15

Champion,

Word of the Day: Faith celebrates ahead of time! Faith comes from focusing on Who is, not what is. Focus on who is your God and what His word says, so what IS does not become your God (that which you are bowing to, that which is controlling you). Live a Life of Faith in God, which produces the fruit of joy, celebration, praise and exuberance. Do not let disappointments or the fear of disappointment quench the fire of faith. When there is a disappointment, declare the truth! All things work together for good for those that love God (Romans 8:28) and I love God, I listen and follow Him and He perfects everything that concerns me (Psalm138:8)and He is making a way where there is no way. He is bringing to pass His good plan in my life (Psalm 37:5 and Jeremiah 29:11). When you are hurt and disappointed don't hurt back. Don't use denial, don't use an ungodly comforter. None of that works, they may bring relief but not victory and definitely no new faith in God. Use the wisdom and strategies of the kingdom and you will experience the kingdom of God's goodness inside and out.

Psalm 37:5 "Commit everything you do to the Lord. Trust Him, and He will help you."

Champion,

HEAR THE HEART of God! Do not be distracted by what other people are doing. Psalm 37:3-9 Trust, lean on, rely on, and be confident in the Lord and do good; so shall you dwell in the land and feed surely on His faithfulness, and truly you shall be fed. Delight yourself also in the Lord, (have a soft and pliable heart not resisting the leadership of our Father but seeking, even hungering for it. Like soft putty seeking to be used.) HE will give you the desires and secret petitions of your heart. Commit your way to the Lord, roll and repose each care of your load on Him; trust, lean on, rely on, and be confident also in Him and HE will bring it to pass. Be still and rest in the Lord; wait for Him and patiently lean yourself upon Him; FRET not yourself ... Cease from anger and forsake wrath; fret not yourself—it tends only to evildoing.

Psalm 37:7-9 "Be still in the presence of the Lord, and wait patiently for Him to act. Don't worry about evil people who prosper or fret about their wicked schemes. Stop being angry! Turn from your rage! Do not lose your temper—it only leads to harm. For the wicked will be destroyed, but those who trust in the Lord will possess the land."

APRIL 17

Champion,

When you revere Him, He steers the ship of your life. And no one knows the way, or can make a way better than Him.

Psalm 37:23-24 "The Lord directs the steps of the godly. He delight in every detail of their lives. Though they stumble, they will never fall, for the Lord holds them by the hand."

Champion,

Ask God to deliver you from the C's and establish you in the E's, Champion! Deliverance from the C's of complaining, criticism and condemning people. And establish you in the E's of edifying, encouraging and exhorting with wisdom and love. This God-given strategy will produce great relationships and great success for everyone, with God saying "well done". That transformation happens when your focus becomes giving instead of getting. Focus on what you're giving to people INSTEAD of what you're NOT getting from them. Ask God to fill your Heart with His Love and Wisdom. Remember, It's your Heavenly Father that will meet all your needs. Put and keep your hope and faith in Him. Not a certain person or particular strategy other then His faithfulness.

Ephesians 4:28 "Don't use foul or abusive language. Let everything you say be good and helpful, so that your words will be an encouragement to those who hear them. And do not bring sorrow to God's Holy Spirit by the way you live. Remember, He has identified you as His own, guaranteeing that you will be saved on the day of redemption."

Champion,

Genuine thankfulness makes a way, and opens doors. Sincere praise causes intimacy and unity.

Psalm 95:2-3 "Let us come to Him with thanksgiving. Let us sing psalms of praise to Him. For the Lords is a great God, and great King above all gods."

APRIL 20

Champion,

Psalm 103:1-5 Bless affectionately, gratefully praise the Lord, O my soul; and all that is deepest within me, bless His holy name! Bless affectionately, gratefully praise the Lord, O my soul, and forget not one of all His benefits. Who forgives every one of all your iniquities, Who heals each one of all your diseases, Who redeems your life from the pit and corruption, Who beautifies, dignifies, and crowns you with loving-kindness and tender mercy; Who satisfies your mouth your necessity and desire at your personal age and situation with good so that your youth, renewed, is like the eagle's strong, overcoming, soaring!

Psalm 103:1-5 "Let all that I am praise the Lord; with my whole heart, I will praise His holy name. Let all that I am praise the Lord; may I never forget the good things He does for me. He forgives all my sins and heals all my diseases. He redeems me from death and crowns me with love and tender mercies. He fills my life with good things."

Champion,

John 8:12 Once more Jesus addressed the crowd. He said,"I am the Light of the world. He who follows Me will not be walking in the dark, but will have the Light, which is Life". -----Now turn that into a declaration -Jesus is the light of the world and I follow Him by His Spirit. He leads me and I walk in the Light with clarity, confidence and courage. I experience the light and the life that Jesus came to give me. I am blessed and I am a blessing, day and night and night and day. Remember; revelation, meditation, declaration, transformation. A believing heart speaks and moves mountains or makes them! You create your world with whatever is in your heart and comes out of your mouth.

John 8:12 "Jesus spoke to the people once more and said, "I am the light of the world. If you follow Me, you won' have to walk in darkness, because you will have the light that leads to life"

Champion,

Romans 8:32 He who did not withhold or spare even His own Son but gave Him up for us all, will He not also with Him freely and graciously give us all other things? Walk by faith not by sight my friend and declare; "Provision is not a problem, my God makes a way, my God shows me the way, my God provides the way and I walk in the way He shows me."

Romans 8:32 "Since He did not spare even His own Son but gave Him up for us all, won't He also give us everything else?"

Champion,

Psalm 100:1-5: "Make a joyful noise to the Lord, all you lands! Serve the Lord with gladness! Come before His presence with singing! Know perceive, recognize, and understand with approval that the Lord is God! It is He Who has made us, not we ourselves and we are His! We are His people and the sheep of His pasture. Enter into His gates with thanksgiving and a thank offering and into His courts with praise! Be thankful and say so to Him, bless and affectionately praise His name! For the Lord is good; His mercy and loving-kindness are everlasting, His faithfulness and truth endure to all generations."

Psalm 47:1 "Come, everyone! Clap your hands! Shout to God with joyful praise!"

Champion,

Protect your heart - An offended heart negatively affects every area of your life. It releases a poison to destroy your relationship with God and your faith in God. It will destroy you mentally, physically, financially and relationally. You are the only one that can do something about it. Ask God to help you be a champion at staying free from being offended and have a healthy heart. You can be your own worst enemy. The devil and people are not the problem; your lack of response to the heart cry of God, to the Wisdom of God is the problem. Remember this simple prescription: ask your Heavenly Father to clean you out and fill you up with His spirit of power, love and wisdom every day all day and you will be strong and not weak, wise and not foolish, loving and not selfish. Having abundant life on the inside destroying works of darkness on the outside.

Psalm 51:10 "Create in me a clean heart, O God. Renew a loyal spirit within me."

Champion,

You are loved. You are loved means you are valuable, you are important and you have something to offer. Provision is not a problem because the one that loves you more than anyone else, The Heavenly Father, will follow through and provide for you. He has destined you to do good works. You are loved means He will meet your needs. You will not be forsaken or forgotten. You are loved means help is available, comfort will be provided. If you call, perfect love responds, answers, understands, is compassionate, patient and kind. YOUR IDENTITY is BELOVED; deeply dearly sincerely genuinely cared for. Meditate on this 3x a day for 5 minutes because the reality of this Love inspires, motivates and strengthens. It is the fuel that makes all the difference.

3 John 1:2 "Dear friend, I hope all is well with you and that you are as healthy in body as you are strong in spirit."

Champion,

Do not be distracted: Remember who loves you more than anybody else, praise Him throughout the day. Take praise breaks and you will be blessed and a blessing.

Psalm 145:14,16,18-19 T"he Lord upholds all those of His own who are falling and rises up all those who are bowed down. You open Your hand and satisfy every living thing with favor. The Lord is near to all who call upon Him, to all who call upon Him sincerely and in truth. He will fulfill the desires of those who reverently and worshipfully fear Him; He also will hear their cry and will save them." (AMP)

Champion,

When following Jesus -The three C's of the devil: criticism, condemnation and contention are determined to destroy and create confusion. The three C's of God: clarity, confidence and courage are designed to give you joy, strength, power and let the authority of God flow out of you. That's the last thing the devil wants. Ask God to help you have the clarity, confidence and courage that you need to follow Jesus all the way, know and imitate Him every day.

2 Timothy 1:7 "For God has not given us a spirit of fear and timidity, but of power, love, and self-discipline."

Champion,

Christianity is not a religion. It is a reality. It is the fruit of saying yes to a living, listening, loving, caring, sharing and lifting out of darkness Heavenly Father, our Heavenly Provider, Almighty God. It is the results of someone loving you more than anybody else, giving His very best, Jesus, so we could experience His goodness. Set your heart on His generosity and ask Him to fill your heart with new love and wisdom. Put all your hope in Him. It will empower you to overcome and be a blessing, which brings Him great pleasure. Let's create a domino effect that Rocks the Nations.

John 15:13 "There is no greater love than to lay down one's life for one's friends."

Champion,

You Can Have Joy Every Day Champion. You don't have to wait for them, they, this or that. Psalm 16:8, 11; I have set the Lord continually before me; set my mind on Him because He is at my right hand, I shall not be moved. You will show me the path of life; in Your Presence is fullness of joy, at Your right hand there are pleasures forevermore. Good news if you are saved, born again His presence is right inside of you, stir it up by thanking Him. Stir it up by being grateful for all that He's already done for you, for Who He is and He will inhabit your praises. His presence will multiply, cleanse and give you fresh Joy. Celebrate! The Greatest of all loves you! You are not alone, He is for You, He is with you, and you are loved not forsaken or forgotten. Celebrate now! You don't have to wait for Friday. When you use God's principles, His wisdom every day could be Friday. Embrace this day with great expectation that something good is going to happen because of who your God is and if it seems like it's not, continue to believe in God's Goodness. Joy is the Fruit of Faith.

Psalm 16:8 & 11 "I know the LORD is always with me. I will not be shaken, for he is right beside me. You will show me the way of life, granting me the joy of your presence and the pleasures of living with you forever."

Champion,

A certain Bible teacher describes wisdom as: God's principles produce abundant life, but if we prefer lawlessness, which is misusing the freedom to do whatever we want to do. We are setting ourselves up for failure and working against the manufacturer's handbook. God created us and He knows what profits and what does not. If we choose the principle of lawlessness ,which is doing what we want, when we want, how we want it without regard to His leadership, we can expect to reap the inevitable results, which include slavery, death, and the loss of privileges or freedoms. This is precisely what happened to the man and woman in the Garden of Eden. Champion ask God to help you operate by His principles that cause goodness to manifest. That is His heart's desire, don't be like Adam and Eve, trust Him, be patient, hold fast, follow through, it will be worth the effort of steadfast faith in Him.

Romans 6:6 "We know that our old sinful selves were crucified with Christ so that sin might lose its power in our lives. We are no longer slaves to sin."

Champion,

Your greatest friend is rejoicing and your greatest enemy is resentment. Focus on the good and you will find it. Look for the good and you will find it. Remember the good and you will remember and be empowered to rejoice and create your own fuel source by the Spirit of God that will strengthen you and empower you the whole day through. Ask God to help you, your Heavenly Father will not fail you but help you sail through instead of suffer through.

Romans 12:2 "Don't copy the behavior and customs of this world, but let God transform you into a new person by changing the way you think. Then you will learn to know God's will for you, which is good and pleasing and perfect."

Champion,

If you live to give instead of to get, you will have all you need and more. You will be un-offendable and very dependable with all that God gives you, a pillar of peace and power. Here is the vision: Born to Bless, Live to Give and Love to Serve the Heart of the Heavenly Father!

Mark 10:45 "For even the Son of Man came not to be served but to serve others and to give his life as a ransom for many."

Champion,

The Lord says: when you put your hope and trust in Him, He will make a way when it looks like there is no way and you will experience more than you could even think or imagine. Say "NO" to the fear of disappointment, my friend, and believe that because the Lord is your shepherd, your leader, your guide and His goodness is going to pursue you and overtake you no matter what it looks like. His good plan is going to manifest in your life.

Psalm 18:32 "God arms me with strength and he makes my way perfect."

Champion,

The Lord says: when it's hard don't swear, declare I can do it by His grace, I can do it by His grace, and I can do it by His grace. Grace is unmerited favor and divine empowerment and it is available 24/7.

2 Corinthians 12:9 "Each time he said, "My grace is all you need. My power works best in weakness." So now I am glad to boast about my weaknesses, so that the power of Christ can work through me."

Champion,

The spirit of prosperity says there's good and plenty for everybody, never a reason to be jealous, but only rejoice when someone else gets blessed. It manifests a generous spirit causing a person to focus on blessing others. Spirit of poverty says hold on, don't let go, why they get it and not me. It causes people to be afraid, angry and depressed. The spirit of prosperity manifests from an attitude of faith in the reality of who Almighty God is and what He has promised. If you want to have FUN today ask God to help you be like Him, follow His lead, follow your heart and give, give, give, love, love, love, bless, bless, bless, serve, serve, serve, honor, honor and honor.

1 Samuel 25:6 "Peace and prosperity to you, your family, and everything you own!"

Champion,

Jeremiah-32:27 BEHOLD, (Focus on me – not on what you see) and Believe. I am the LORD, (supreme authority) the God of all flesh; is anything too difficult for Me? (I am the master mechanic I can fix the bodies that I created) Isaiah 45:2 I will go before you and level the mountains to make the crooked places straight; I will break in pieces the doors of bronze and cut asunder the bars of iron. Jer.29:11 -For I know the plans I have for you," declares the Lord, "plans to prosper you and not to harm you, plans to give you hope and a future. Activate your faith in Almighty God, my friends and don't let the fear of disappointment stop you. Love for people and faith in our Father is enough it will move mountains and destroy the works of evil.

Isaiah 45:2 "This is what the LORD says: I will go before you, Cyrus, and level the mountains. I will smash down gates of bronze and cut through bars of iron."

My friend,

When You appreciate, you "appreciate" in value, When you appreciate others, others appreciate in value within themselves. When you appreciate others publicly, their value appreciates to those listening. When you and I don't appreciate, everything is depreciated in value, even if it's valuable. Ask the Father to help you be consistently appreciative. It will cause health instead of death.

Proverbs 18:21 "Death and life are in the power of the tongue, And those who love it and indulge it will eat its fruit and bear the consequences of their words." (AMP)

Champion,

Mothers were created by God and are loved by God and the Heavenly Father loves all the mothers. Honor your mother this week. Find out what would bless her...and do it.

Proverbs 31: 28-29 "Her children stand and bless her. Her husband praises her: "There are many virtuous and capable women in the world, but you surpass them all!"

Champions 21 Day Challenge

Psalm 23

1 The Lord is my shepherd;
I have all that I need.
2 He lets me rest in green meadows;
He leads me beside peaceful streams.
3   He renews my strength.
He guides me along right paths,
bringing honor to his name.
4 Even when I walk
through the darkest valley,[a]
I will not be afraid,
for you are close beside me.
Your rod and your staff
protect and comfort me.
5 You prepare a feast for me
in the presence of my enemies.
You honor me by anointing my head with oil.
My cup overflows with blessings.
6 Surely your goodness and unfailing love will pursue me
all the days of my life,
and I will live in the house of the Lord
forever.
(BOOKMARK THIS PAGE)

Champion,

Luke 6:45 Whatever you store in your heart, comes out of your mouth. Proverbs 18:21 says "Death and life are in the power of the tongue, and they who indulge in it shall eat the fruit of it for death or life." Dr. Caroline leaf, in her new book, "Switch on your Brain," explains based on research that it takes three cycles of 21 days for the rest of your life to renew your mind to make sure what you are speaking is producing life . In her 21 day Brain Detox Plan, she teaches how to use 7 to 10 minutes daily. Use Psalm 23 every morning for 21 days starting today. Soak your heart in it and then declare it over your future and you will be planting seeds that will produce a very profitable harvest."

DAY 1
(SEE MAY 9TH FOR PSALM 23)

Champion,

Let's advance together by using the wisdom of God found in Joshua 1:8 Meditate (Think and speak) the word of God day and night, making sure you practice everything written in it. Then you'll get where you're going; then you'll succeed. Haven't I commanded you strength and courage! Don't be timid; don't get discouraged. God, your God, is with you every step you take." Meditate on Psalm 23 for new victory and to be a greater blessing to others.

DAY 2
(SEE MAY 9TH FOR PSALM 23)

Champion,

Like your Heavenly Father, you create with your mouth, so download the upgraded program of God's word into your heart and speak it! It will stop the work of the enemy and release the power and resources of God to bring into manifestation His good plan for your life! Permeate your heart and practice with your mouth Psalm 23 and you will see what I mean.

DAY 3
(SEE MAY 9TH FOR PSALM 23)

Champion,

Complaining is a mis-use of your energy and time! It is unprofitable and unproductive. In doing this you are cooperating with the destroyer. Drink and eat Psalm 23 and use it as your declaration! You will see a new manifestation. If you continue in faith and patience something good will happen. Do not BACK DOWN or SLOW DOWN because you are called to MOW DOWN the works of darkness!

DAY 4
(SEE MAY 9TH FOR PSALM 23)

Champion,

Day Five : This 21 day exercise/opportunity is designed to take you out of survive and into thrive for your benefit and the benefit of others! So don't despise, but value and follow through. Keep watering and weeding your heart with Psalm 23! You are a victor not a victim and you have the opportunity to triumph through Jesus Christ! So stand up and fight the good fight of faith and speak the word of God, You will be found moving mountains instead of being moved by them.

DAY 5
(SEE MAY 9TH FOR PSALM 23)

Champion,

Champion, day six and you're putting the devil in a fix! He is starting to sweat because he can tell that this strategy from God is making a difference in your heart. He can hear it in your voice. Continue with Psalm 23 and don't wait for somebody else or something else, JUST DO IT! Fill up with the water of the word and be a super soaker that drowns the enemy!

DAY 6
(SEE MAY 9TH FOR PSALM 23)

Champion,

Day seven is designed by God to get you to higher ground. Higher ground for sheep always represented a place of plenty! He is near so let's give Him the gift of faithfulness and follow through with this strategy, it's a win-win situation! I believe in this season there will be great testimonies from using what He has been giving us. When you testify, remember that others will be encouraged because of it! You will set others free from hope-lessness and unbelief, because your testimony will let them know that life is worth living and the Lord will do awesome things for them too!!

DAY 7
(SEE MAY 9TH FOR PSALM 23)

Champion,

The apostle Paul said war a good warfare with the word of God that has been given to you, fill the gun of your heart with the bullets of Psalm 23 and fire away! You are doing great on day number eight!

DAY 8
(SEE MAY 9TH FOR PSALM 23)

Champion,

Trust in the perfect love of God and put on the garment of praise! Start thanking God for all the benefits of the Lord being your shepherd! This is day nine, see if you can find nine things in Psalm 23 to thank him for!

DAY 9
(SEE MAY 9TH FOR PSALM 23)

Champion,

One of meanings of number 10 in the Bible represents divine order. This is day 10 and the Lord wants you to renew your mind so that it is controlled by His Word, not the world of your circumstances. So continue to soak your heart in Psalm 23 so there will be divine order inside of you and words that create order coming out of your heart!

DAY 10
(SEE MAY 9TH FOR PSALM 23)

Champion,

The purpose of Christian leadership is to equip God's people and fully develop them so that they can know God personally and be overcomers. Then we can help others experience this also! This 21 day strategy has been given to benefit you, but you will never know the value unless you embrace it, I believe that you are, but just in case you have any doubt, hear the heart of God! I don't want you to miss out, this exercise will help you greatly! On day 11 and God wants you to taste and see heaven so you can be free of all ungodly leaven!

DAY 11
(SEE MAY 9TH FOR PSALM 23)

MAY 21

Champion,

Today is day 12 and you are more than halfway there Champion! The word of the Lord says that God watches over His word to perform it, this is good reason to declare His word! Watch Him perform the miraculous in your life and the lives of others!

DAY 12
(SEE MAY 9TH FOR PSALM 23)

Champion,

Every flavor of Gods favor is waiting for you! The throne of grace is like an ice cream parlor, every flavor of His favor has been paid for by Jesus. The Heavenly Father loves you more than anyone else, so approach the Throne of Grace like a child approaches an ice cream counter and knows every flavor is available and already paid for. All they have to do is ask with thankfulness and appreciation. Ask Him for the flavor favor of the day, He knows the one you need the most.

DAY 13
(SEE MAY 9TH FOR PSALM 23)

Champion,

Jesus is the one that will delight you and excite you! He knows you better than you know yourself! Psalm 23 is true, and if you follow the great Shepherd Jesus, His goodness will pursue you and overtake you. Exercise your faith and declare. Call those things that are not as though they were. You have the power and permission!

DAY 14
(SEE MAY 9TH FOR PSALM 23)

Champion,

Every day you're writing a page in the book of your life! What is it going to say? Will it say that you gave up or rose up? If you've given your heart to Jesus, you have resurrection power on the inside of you, so stir it up right now and declare Psalm 23. Continue in thanks and praise to God for His goodness on this 15th day of Gods' empowering strategy!

DAY 15
(SEE MAY 9TH FOR PSALM 23)

Champion,

Jesus is the "link" that you are looking for. The more you believe that and draw near privately and publicly, the more convinced you will be. Then you will experience more faith, abundant life, and peace. The strategy of satan is to keep you from that "link" and the gathering place He has called you to because this is that which helps and enables you too experience Him and the support of His people.

DAY 16
(SEE MAY 9TH FOR PSALM 23)

Champion,

If you will embrace your problems with faith and believe that something good is going to come out of them, you will grow and receive your promotion! Being irritated, frustrated and offended is just a sign that you're not overcoming. Remember, hard things like problems, people, etc. are like barbells in the gym. They are designed to make you stronger and if you embrace them with faith in your Gods integrity knowing that He is with you and for you, something good is going to come out of it. So Thank God for the problems, He promises double for your trouble! You will have wisdom, strength, and rewards for rejoicing instead of resenting. New peace and new joy will be the results, as well as new health and prosperity according to the Proverbs.

DAY 17
(SEE MAY 9TH FOR PSALM 23)

Champion,

Faith celebrates ahead of time, focused on the Fathers integrity because He says what He means and means what He says! He will make a way! His hand is NOT short, but mighty, and ALL things are possible for those who believe, so be encouraged and stand up night and day, and declare the Lord is my shepherd and He will show you the way!

DAY 18
(SEE MAY 9TH FOR PSALM 23)

Champion,

Make the decision today and keep on making it, that no matter what happens, praise will come out of your mouth! Know that honoring God is your highest priority! Knowing that and flowing with Him, imitating the Father and Jesus by the power of the Holy Spirit, and walking by faith and love are the Greatest HAVE TO's of your life! THEN you will be unshakable, unmovable and un-offendable. You will be at the right place at the right time and you will experience the goodness of God like never before! You will walk in peace and power that devours every strategy of satan that is designed to steal and destroy your destiny and the destiny of those whose lives you touch! Align with the Divine my Friends, you will have an amazing life and hear the Father say "well done."

DAY 19
(SEE MAY 9TH FOR PSALM 23)

Champion,

Recognize that many times we are putting reliance on natural things such as insurance companies or natural circumstances. Instead, have faith in the Supernatural Kingdom Company of The Father, Son, and Holy Ghost! Do not be controlled by what has happened but declare what IS going to happen because the Lord is your Shepherd. Don't back down because of what you see and don't let circumstances change your declaration. Say no to the spirit of fear and the what ifs so you can declare what is! Declare Gods' word and what's going to happen in your future.

DAY 20
(SEE MAY 9TH FOR PSALM 23)

Champion,

Hope you have been excited by the truth of Psalm 23, because when the Lord is your Shepherd, you know that something good is going to happen today! When it looks like that's not true, hang onto Romans 8:28 and declare: the Lord is MY shepherd and ALL things will work together for my good! It will, because God will come through for you because of who HE is. Because of His Integrity you can have expectancy. Sheep always made the leading of their shepherd their highest priority, because they knew if they stayed close, kept their eyes set on him, listened for his voice and followed him, everything they needed would be provided for. The Shepherd always had their best interest at heart and He does the same for you today!

MAY 31

Champion,

Set your affections on Him, make HIM your highest priority and dwell in the secret place of the Most High, which is His Presence! You can continually cultivate and freshen up through thanksgiving and praise and you will find relief from the stresses of life! If you do this throughout the day, you will go to bed with testimonies of his faithfulness, excited to wake up the next day and experience Him all over again.

Isaiah 50:4 "The sovereign Lord has given me His words of wisdom, so that I know how to comfort the weary. Morning by morning He wakens me and opens my understanding to His will."

Champion,

God says, It's time to be healed, it's time to be restored, it's time to be released into the fullness of your destiny. He says I am here to rescue you! Reach out, cry out and I will lift you out!

2 Corinthians 6:2 "For God says, "At just the right time, I heard you. On the day of salvation, I helped you. " Indeed the "right time" is now. Today is the day of salvation."

Champion,

It's a good morning and a great day to be a blessing and to bless others with Gods presence and His love from your heart. Remember every day.... GAME ON! LOVE! LOOSE! LIFT! I release new grace to erase the works of darkness, to pursue and recover all, to rescue, restore and release into new peace the people that you meet today! Arise to be the champion that you are by the grace of God, for the glory of God.

Genesis 12:2 "I will make you into a great nation. I will bless you and make you famous, and you will be a blessing to others."

Champion,

The Lord says covet Me, The Greatest Treasure of All! Covet means to wish for, long for, and to crave for something! Remember His presence provides Fullness of Joy. Fullness that nothing can touch is waiting for you, every moment of every day there is power, love, wisdom, clarity, peace, strength, and abundant life from the inside out-Enjoy!!

Psalms 16:11 "You will show me the way of life, granting me the joy of Your presence and the Pleasures of living with You forever."

Champion,

You can either live in the grip of regret or soar in the spirit of faith! Jeremiah 29:11 is true, God has a hope and a future for me!!, no matter what it looks like or what has happened!

Proverbs 10:28 "The hope of the (uncompromisingly) righteous (the upright, en right standing with Goda0 is gladness, but the expectation of the wicked (those who are out of harmony with God) comes for nothing." (AMP)

Champion,

Watch out! Quarreling is quicksand, and arguing is fear-based communication. It is lack of love, faith and wisdom in action! It DESTROYS! It is a consuming plague. STOP, shut up, and pray, pray, pray, do not stay, get away quickly! If you cannot process in peace ,you are on the wrong path, headed for the rocks at the bottom of the cliff!! Ask God to fill you with New Life and there will be no more strife.

Proverbs 15:1 "A gentle answer deflects anger, but harsh words make tempers flare."

Champion,

The Lord says, many people are committing suicide on a daily basis through their thought life, they are killing themselves. Cast your cares to the One that cares for you more than anyone else can. Cast down evil imaginations that distract, destroy and depress you with His help.

1 Peter 5:7 "Give all your worries and cares to God, for He cares for you."

Champion,

God is forgiving, gracious and kind! Arise and do not despise the grace and Glory of God today! This is the day, beautiful, powerful things are going to happen today!

Nehemiah 9:17b "But You are a God of forgiveness, gracious and merciful, slow to become angry, and rich in unfailing love."

Champion,

Remember, thoughts are seeds that either cause weeds or trees. Weeds of death or trees of life. This is a result of what you are meditating on, on a daily basis.

Psalm 1:1 "Oh, the joys of those who do not follow the advice of the wicked, or stand around with sinners, or join in with mockers. But they delight in the law of the Lord, meditating on it day and night. They are like TREES planted along the riverbank bearing fruit each season."

Champion,

The reason rejection that comes through betrayal and abandonment is so devastating is because acceptance is so powerful. Here is the good news! When you say yes to Jesus, He becomes the door of acceptance and God says "Come on in, you are welcome, you are wanted, and I love you." You do not have to be perfect to be accepted....Just BELIEVE the good news!

John 14:6 "Jesus told him, "I am the way, the truth, and the life, no one can come to the Father except through Me"

JUNE 10

Champion,

Do not restrict love for poor performance, just speak the truth in love to help the person blossom into their potential!

Ephesians 4:15 "Instead, we will speak the truth in love, growing in every way more and more like Christ, who is the head of His body, the church."

Champion,

God says if you seek Him, you will find Him, and the more you find Him the more you will know Him and the more you know Him the more you will love Him; and that changes EVERYTHING for the better. For in His Presence is Fullness of Joy!

Psalm 27:4 "The one thing I ask for, the one thing I seek the most- is to live in the house of the Lord all the days of my life, delighting in the Lord's perfections, and meditating in His temple."

JUNE 12

Champion,

Trying harder does not work. It causes us to focus on ourselves, on our strength and efforts. It's something that we have been taught without knowing, to save us from the pain of condemnation, shame, and the pain of failure. It's something that we have used to gain acceptance and the attention of others. Instead fix your eyes on Jesus today!

Isaiah 26:3,4 "You will keep in perfect peace all who trust in You, all whose thoughts are fixed on You."

Champion,

God says it's time to shed the shackles of fear, shame and guilt and be delivered of every wound of rejection, condemnation and exasperation by responding to His invitation for new freedom today! THIS is the day, not someday, this is the Day! BELIEVE ME and CRY OUT!!

John 8:32,36 "And you will know the truth, and the truth will set you free.....So if the Son sets you free, you are truly free!"

JUNE 14

Champion,

Do not channel surf. Keep your mind set on God and you will hear His voice every day. There is nothing more exciting!

Colossians 3:1,2 "Since you have been raised to a new life with Christ, set your sights on the realities of heaven, where Christ sits in the place of honor at God's right hand. Think about the things of heaven, not the things of earth."

Champion,

I hope you read this, because it may be for you or someone you know. On this Father's Day, the Greatest of all wants you to know that HE understands and that HE is the only one that can heal, relieve, and set you free from the deep heart pain that you are carrying. He wants you to stop relying on certain people that you think should understand because that will only increase the pain. Draw near to Him and give Him all the anguish, internal turmoil, hurt, anger, fear and pain. If you open your heart, He will clean every part you will receive compassion, kindness, patience and the burden will be removed. New peace and joy awaits you!

Psalm 28:7 "The Lord is my strength and shield. I trust him with all my heart. He helps me, and my heart is filled with joy. I burst out in songs of thanksgiving."

Champion,

People that have been wounded by rejection and are not healed, carry and walk in an orphan spirit. This invisible force repels the very love and acceptance that their heart desires. Because of this their hearts are starving to death, making them angry and blaming other people and even God for their condition. The GOOD NEWS is God sent Jesus to heal the brokenhearted. Ask Him to do a complete work in you and the others around you.

Isaiah 61:1 "The Spirit of the Sovereign Lord is upon me, for the Lord has anointed me to bring good news to the poor. He has sent me to comfort the brokenhearted and to proclaim that captives will be released and prisoners will be freed."

Champion,

Good morning! Remember, as God's people we have been given today to impact tomorrow, every little and big thing you do today is a seed that produces something tomorrow, good or bad. The Apostle Paul encourages us to do the profitable thing, so help us, Holy Spirit, to do the profitable thing!

Galatians 6:7 "Don't be mislead, you cannot mock the justice of God. You will always harvest what you plant."

Champion,

Champions don't give up, they GET UP! They don't make excuses, they SEEK SOLUTIONS!

Psalm 119:32 "I will pursue Your commands, for You expand my understanding."

Champion,

God says it's time to arise and to despise every reason, every fear, and every excuse that is keeping you in the mediocrity of a life without fiery purpose and passion. He's saying to follow Him like you never have before! Respond to Him NOW. Say here I am Lord, I give You my heart, I give You my life! Come on Champions! CRY OUT and receive your upgrade today!!

Isaiah 60:1 "Arise Jerusalem! Let your light shine for all too see. For the glory of the Lord rises to shine on you."

JUNE 20

Champion,

Regretting and resenting produces death and bondage. Ask Your Heavenly Father to set you free from both ungodly patterns that only result in misery and depression. Ask Him to help you follow His scriptural prescriptions. The results are amazing and you will experience abundant life from the inside out. 1 Thessalonians 5:18-19 "Give thanks in all circumstances; for this is the will of God in Christ Jesus for you." Do Not Quench The Spirit.

1 Peter 5:6-7 "Humble yourselves, therefore, under the mighty hand of God so that at the proper time he may exalt you, casting all your anxieties on him, because he cares for you."

Psalm 118:24 "This is the day that the Lord has made; let us rejoice and be glad in it."

Champion,

ONCE more the Spirit of God says "I Want you!", "I Love You!" "I am Here for You!" "Receive ME NOW!", "I will refresh you", "I will strengthen you like Nothing Else that Exists. SAY THIS - "SPIRIT of the Living God, fill me up, clean me out, fill me up, clean me out, fill me up-TODAY-TODAY-TODAY!!!"

Proverbs 11:25 "The generous will prosper; those who re-fresh others will themselves be refreshed."

Champion,

God says He wants to clean out all the plaque from the attacks against your heart, so that NEW LIFE would pulsate, permeate and penetrate your whole being. Say yes, open up your heart to Him and you will be glad you did.

2 Corinthians 6:13 "I am asking you to respond as if you were my own children. Open your hearts to us!"

Champion,

Unhealed offenses create fences in your heart. When you feel offended we need God to mend us. Pray, pray, pray and ask God to help you. Pray for more love, more wisdom and more power. You may not have to say anything but if you do, it will produce more good when you process with God first.

Psalm 116:1 "I love the Lord because he hears my voice and my prayer for mercy."

Champion,

Your meditation matters! You are either releasing life, death, medicine or poison into your system by what you are thinking about. You are the fruit of your focus. You manifest according to your meditation, you are either free or bound according to the condition of your heart. Your soul, (mind, will & emotions), prosperity should be your top priority.

Deuteronomy 30:15 "Now listen! Today I am giving you a choice between life and death, between prosperity and disaster."

Champion,

Chew on this for lunch. God LIKES YOU, that's right God LIKES YOU, He would not have sent Jesus unless HE liked you, take advantage of His kindness, his generosity and receive the truth. Remember He is not in the game of Shame that's the devil's voice, his voice does not condemn, it releases us from condemnation. Remember you are good, even when your behavior is bad. He hates poor choices because they can destroy us."

Romans 4:18 " Even when there was no reason for hope, Abraham kept hoping—believing that he would become the father of many nations..."

Champion,

Like slivers in our fingers that come from handling wood, so slivers get in our heart from handling life. Slivers that are not removed can cause a dangerous infection and so can slivers in the heart. There is a surgeon that loves you. He is the only one that can remove the slivers by His Spirit. Ask Him to remove those slivers, that you may be found fully alive!

2 Corinthians 3:17 "For the Lord is the Spirit, and wherever the Spirit of the Lord is, there is freedom."

Champion,

A wounded heart leads to a broken spirit and wrong thinking. That keeps you drinking, the poison of your wrong thinking. Quickly, ask God to rescue your wounded heart, restore your broken spirit, renew your mind ,so you can be and do all that he is called you to. Soar not snore in the bed of affliction.

Romans 12:22 "Don't copy the behavior and customs of this world, but let God transform you into a new person by changing the way you think. Then you will learn to know God's will for you, which is good and pleasing and perfect."

Champion,

The root of all evil is the love of comforts; that is, OUR own comfort, without considering God's ways or other people's heart. That's why God said love Him first, He knows it's the guard rail to keep you from the ditch of evil.

Deuteronomy 6:5 "And you must love the Lord your God with all your heart, all your soul, and all your strength."

Champion,

Choose forgiveness right away or you will be found drowning and frowning. Then pray for the person quickly or you will be found sickly!

Luke 17:4 "Even if that person wrongs you seven times a day and each time turns again and asks forgiveness, you must forgive."

Champion,

Many times people do not reach out for help because they're living with pain . Subconsciously they are thinking something is wrong with them because of the rejection they have gone through. So if they reach out for help and admit they have a problem, they feel vulnerable and open to be rejected or hurt again. They think they may be told that they are the problem and the thought of experiencing that pain is unbearable. The heart is a fragile thing especially when wounded. Ask God to heal it, he is the only one that can.

Psalm 62:8 "O my people, trust in him at all times. Pour out your heart to him, for God is our refuge."

Champion,

Remember your meditation matters ,it either scatters the enemy or invites him in, poisons you or medicates you. Ask God to help you think upon the dawn . It produces light and life in your heart, remember He is with you, HE is for You!! It is never about your goodness it is always about His .

1 John 1:7 "But if we are living in the light, as God is in the light, then we have fellowship with each other, and the blood of Jesus, his Son, cleanses us from all sin."

July 2

Champion,

If your meditation is on what God Has done, (even if you have to go all the way back to the cross), the proof of His love, you will have no problem living in expectation of experiencing his goodness. Now, no matter what it looks like, remember what you focus on strengthens you, or weakens you.

Psalm 116:5 "How kind the Lord is! How good he is! So merciful, this God of ours!"

Champion,

If expectation of God's goodness is difficult for you ,increase the supplements of proper meditation .Focus on his nature and ask Him to heal you from the wounds of the past.

Psalm 145:17 "The Lord is righteous in everything he does; he is filled with kindness."

Champion,

Hear the heart of God. He likes you, He loves you, He wants you. He is not mad at you, activate the power of those truths, by repeating them out loud yourself and be nourished by them. Just like an every day utensil or tool or even food, has potential, but never makes a difference until we pick it up and use it.

Hebrews 10:22 "Let us go right into the presence of God with sincere hearts fully trusting him. For our guilty consciences have been sprinkled with Christ's blood to make us clean, and our bodies have been washed with pure water."

Champion,

HEAR the Heart of God- He likes you -He loves you- He wants you -He is not mad at you! Activate the power of those truths, but it will never make a difference until we pick it up and use it.

Ephesians 3:17 "Then Christ will make his home in your hearts as you trust in him. Your roots will grow down into God's love and keep you strong."

Champion,

Rise up and say no to the spirit of fear and yes to the spirit of love and faith that comes from him. Say God is with me, He is for me, He is leading me ,He is helping me. God likes me, He loves me, You create your world with your words.

Lunchtime nugget, acronym for God,

G-great ,O-opportunity , D-daily.

Jeremiah 29:11 "God has a good plan, a good future ,and a hope for you."

Champion,

Here is a highly recommended prayer; "Father in Heaven, help me to imitate and demonstrate your goodness, more and more every single day, so that others would taste and see and know you, trust you and fall in love with you. In Jesus name, amen."

Psalm 136:2 "Give thanks to the God of gods. His faithful love endures forever."

Champion,

The greatest maturity for a Christian is when you can say in the midst of false accusation, mistreatment, and out right wrong behavior , father forgive them for they know not what they do. Just like Jesus did on the cross. Remember it is spiritual forces that are your problem not people .

Colossians 3:13 "Make allowance for each other's faults, and forgive anyone who offends you. Remember, the Lord forgave you, so you must forgive others."

Champion,

Hasty decisions can cause waste and make things worse, so be aware. Take time with your Heavenly Father and share with others involved. Never jump out of hurt, fear and anger. Pray first ,then act.

1 Kings 8:28 "Nevertheless, listen to my prayer and my plea, O Lord my God. Hear the cry and the prayer that your servant is making to you today."

Champion,

Curious people seek, courageous people follow. Ask him to help you find and follow him every moment of every day. There is no pleasure greater! Trust me, then the weather in your heart will be sunny and will determine your day. Remember the wise pay attention and the foolish don't.

Proverbs 17:22 "A cheerful heart is good medicine, but a broken spirit saps a person's strength."

Champion,

Resentment is the fruit of being seduced into a self-focus. It's about what I'm going through and how much I'm suffering, and also what I am doing and what they are not doing. Push the eject button quickly by saying, "God, help me!" Get out of that airplane. It's headed for a deadly crash.

Psalm 69:29 "I am suffering and in pain. Rescue me, O God, by your saving power."

Champion,

Remember the goodness of God and be ignited with praise.
You will be amazed at what happens!

Psalm 16:2 "I said to the LORD, "You are my Master! Every good thing I have comes from you."

Champion,

God's presence meets and exceeds all of your heart's needs. Find a solitary place, then enter the throne of grace with an attitude of thanksgiving and praise and he will raise you to a new level of joy, peace, wisdom and strength. Much love is waiting to fit you like a glove.

Psalm 100:4 "Enter his gates with thanksgiving; go into his courts with praise. Give thanks to him and praise his name."

Champion,

Remember, anyone fretting has stopped relying and has forgotten who God is and that His nature is perfect faithfulness. He has integrity. He means what He says and says what He means. He says that He will help you. You do not have to be afraid. We have forgotten His ability. He makes a way where there is no way. Let these things be what you think upon and peace will manifest.

Philippians 1:6 "And I am certain that God, who began the good work within you, will continue his work until it is finally finished on the day when Christ Jesus returns."

Champion,

The Lord says, "I am the only coping mechanism that leads to life and not bondage." Be free, be blessed!

1 Peter 5:7 "Give all your worries and cares to God, for he cares about you."

Champion,

Talk to the Father. He wants to help you. Pursue his heart. Kindness and generosity, wisdom and strength are available right now. Open your heart and experience the forever Father; the friend you've been looking for. There is no one greater and nothing better. Step into the shower of his presence and be refreshed!

Proverbs 21:21 "Whoever pursues righteousness and unfailing love will find life, righteousness, and honor."

Champion,

Ask God to give you the courage to choose life as well as the courage to ask Him which way is life in every situation. Ask for the courage to walk it out and know true freedom, true joy and liberation from the spirit of fear controlling you. Arise and shine! You have been crowned with glory and honor if you have chosen Jesus.

Deuteronomy 30:19 "Today I have given you the choice between life and death, between blessings and curses. Now I call on heaven and earth to witness the choice you make. Oh, that you would choose life, so that you and your descendants might live!"

Champion,

Remember a prosperous soul and healthy heart respond to problems with peace because faith, hope, love and wisdom are inside. If that's not happening, be honest. Do not blame the other person or situation outside of you. Your reaction is based on what's inside of you. So say, "God, help me!" The Holy Spirit will help you.

Luke 6:45 "A good person produces good things from the treasury of a good heart, and an evil person produces evil things from the treasury of an evil heart. What you say flows from what is in your heart."

Champion,

Make a great day, don't wait for one. Serve, bless, and love others. Wisdom says it's more of a blessing to give than receive. Ask God how you can bless Him. Ask people how you can bless them.

Acts 20:35 "And I have been a constant example of how you can help those in need by working hard. You should remember the words of the Lord Jesus: "It is more blessed to give than to receive."

JULY 20

Champion,

Put all your hope in the One that loves you more than anyone else and proved it on the cross. Any other foundation is a trap door, not a solid floor.

Psalm 39:7 "And so, Lord, where do I put my hope? My only hope is in you."

Champion,

Put your hope in God. Give Him your heart and don't back down, stand down or back-off. Keep exercising your faith constantly, believing that because of his gigantic kindness, His goodness will pursue you and overtake you. Give him the pleasure of believing in Him. It thrills Him when we trust Him.

Psalm 23:6 "Surely your goodness and unfailing love will pursue me all the days of my life, and I will live in the house of the LORD forever."

Champion,

Your lips, mouth, tongue, words, and speech are a reflection of your internal condition. They produce life or death. They help or hurt. Ask God for internal health for your heart, mind and spirit. Your words produce your world.

2 Samuel 23:2 "The Spirit of the LORD speaks through me; his words are upon my tongue."

Champion,

When and where there is anxiety and arguing, nobody is relying on God. Nobody is remembering his wisdom. Humility and reverence for Him produces life, honor and provision. Remember, pursue peace, not strife. Strife opens the door to every other evil.

Proverbs 22:4 "True humility and fear of the LORD lead to riches, honor, and long life."

Champion,

Remember, spirit-soul hygiene is more important than physical hygiene. Cleanse and fill yourself with God's presence and words of life and you will overcome. The toxins that create a bad attitude will destroy your life quicker then the toxins that create body odor.

Psalm 19:12 "How can I know all the sins lurking in my heart? Cleanse me from these hidden faults."

Champion,

Repetition is the mother of all learning. Review yesterday's message.

Deuteronomy 6:6-7   "And you must commit yourselves wholeheartedly to these commands that I am giving you today. Repeat them again and again to your children. Talk about them when you are at home and when you are on the road, when you are going to bed and when you are getting up."

Champion,

Live an energized life! Don't resent -rejoice! Don't deny- rely!
Don't regret- invest now! Don't let evil thoughts in-cast down!
Don't sulk -praise! Don't wander -set your mind! Don't focus on
your weakness -focus on His strength! Don't say I can't -say He
can! Don't look down -look up! Remember what He's done and
that nothing is too hard for Him. Don't think about what you can't
do- think about what He can do. Stay between the lines. Rely-
don't try.

Psalm 100:5 "For the LORD is good. His unfailing love continues forever, and his faithfulness continues to each generation."

Champion,

You will not be a Champion or an overcomer unless you first and foremost comforter is Jesus. Unless your go-to person, your go-to presence, your go-to substance is Jesus, you will experience death instead of life, frustration instead peace and loss instead of gain. You will be empty instead of full. Abundant life awaits you. Ask God to help you choose Jesus at every turn. Check in with Him. He wants to be your everyday Lord and leader, not just your Sunday Savior. He is the wisdom of God and He wants to fill you and bless you. He is a fountain of living water, nothing else will quench your thirst like Him.

Psalm 16:11 "You will show me the way of life, granting me the joy of your presence and the pleasures of living with you forever."

Champion,

If our greatest excitement is not the presence of Jesus and His wisdom, we have not experienced the true presence and wisdom of Jesus, or not enough of it. And we have put something lesser and unprofitable in its place, or are carrying a wound that is quenching our joy for Jesus. Whether that's somebody you know or it's you, ask for a supernatural turn around so we don't break His heart by choosing another comforter.

John 14:16 "And I will ask the Father, and he will give you another Advocate (comforter), who will never leave you."

My friend,

Choosing life, choosing Jesus, is not a one time event that leads to abundant life. It is a moment by moment, nano-second decision of doing what you know is right in His sight. And He sees everything. Abundant life first and foremost is having a clear conscience, having a confidence that you are bringing Him pleasure by putting Him first. Relying and trusting in Him, which produces abundant life from the inside out. He is pleased because He knows that if you follow Him, you will experience the Destiny He has for you, and help others experience the same. He is the Answer. Because He has all the answers to all your questions. Don't let anything in this world keep you from seeking, knowing and flowing with Him.

John 10:10 "The thief 's purpose is to steal and kill and destroy. My purpose is to give them a rich and satisfying life."

Champion,

The experts told me to clean out my iPhone often, from all the different uses or apps that I opened during the day, otherwise what's hidden, what's unseen will drain the battery. I find the same thing is true concerning people's hearts. The wisdom of God is very helpful, it says cast all your cares on to the Lord, because He wants to help you. Ask Him to help you clean out your heart. Ask Him to take all the junk that is hidden and unseen; hurt, fear, anger, bitterness, unforgiveness and offenses. Remember, denial leads to death, truth leads to freedom. Choose forgiveness and pray for yourself and other people, to be like Jesus.

Psalm 51:10 "Create in me a clean heart, O God. Renew a loyal spirit within me."

Champion,

What you revere ,steers. What you value the most controls you. The Greatest of all, promises you in Proverbs 10:27 that revering Him first and foremost prolongs your days. No one loves you more than Jesus and His Father. No one or anything else deserves first place more than Him. Ask Him to help you value Him more than anything else. He wants to see you free and flourishing.

Proverbs 10:27 "Fear of the Lord lengthens one's life, but the years of the wicked are cut short."

AUGUST 1

Champion,

Good news! You have the Answer! You have the Answer that leads to all the answers. If you have given your heart and your life to Jesus, you are one with the One that knows everything. He owns everything and provides everything, all you have to do is call on the Name of the Lord and you will be saved, helped, rescued, restored and redeemed. No one loves you more! If you give your whole heart, your whole life to Him, you will experience a significant life, with great rewards now and forever.

Romans 10:9-10 "If you openly declare that Jesus is Lord and believe in your heart that God raised Him for the dead, you will be saved. For it is by believing in your heart that you are made right with God, and it is by openly declaring your faith that you are saved."

Champion,

Significant One, Relationship is a dynamic, designed by God, to help you. There are many kinds of relationships. If we use God's wisdom, they will help you experience abundant life. Or without God they can lead you astray. Whether it be a relationship with money, a person, a substance, food, object or pet. The reason that Jesus has asked to be first, your first love, your first comforter, your leader or your bodyguard is because He will help you stay free, and not get stuck to anything that will cause you to miss out on His Goodness.

Matthew 6:33 "Seek the Kingdom of God above all else, and live righteously, and He will give you everything you need."

Champion,

God is a rewarder of those who diligently seek Him and follow Him. No one loves you more than Jesus. Draw near and stay near, so you taste and see His goodness. Because of what He has "Already Done" you always have a reason to celebrate, which leads to constant refreshing, new strength and wisdom.

Hebrews 11:6 "It is impossible to please God without faith. Anyone who wants to come to Him must believe that God exists and that He rewards those who sincerely seek Him."

Champion,

The throne room of grace is open 24/7. And the Promise Maker and Keeper says as a Christian, a child of God, we can enter and get the help that we need. What do you need? Wisdom, clarity, love, peace, joy and kindness. New strength, faith, hope, and new understanding. Enter with thanksgiving for what He's already done. Draw near and revere the One that loves you more than anyone else. The results are amazing.

Hebrews 10:19-20 "And so, dear brothers and sisters, we can boldly enter heaven's Most Holy Place because of the blood of Jesus. By His death, Jesus opened a new and life-giving way through the curtain into the Most Holy Place."

Champion,

Jesus came to create order because Adam and Eve created disorder by not remaining faithful and trusting God. Sin created disorder and chaos. Righteousness, creates order , peace and joy by the power of the Holy Spirit. The Holy Spirit is like a great chiropractor, mechanic, tradesmen, teacher or anyone else that brings alignment which produces abundant life. That's why the devil doesn't want people to follow Jesus, remain faithful to Him, and imitate Him. The devil wants to destroy people. Jesus wants people to experience abundant life, that's why He came. Stay grateful and faithful you will be glad you did. The rewards are amazing. And if you fall away, return quickly. Mercy is waiting for you.

1 John 1: 9 "But is we confess our sins to Him, He is faithful and just to forgive us our sins and to cleanse us from all wickedness."

Champion,

No One wants to help you more, no one loves you more, no one values you more, no one has done more for you, than Jesus!! He is the answer that leads to every answer. He's available right now. Seek and you will find, the results are amazing!!

Luke 11:9 "And so I tell you, keep on asking, and you will receive what you ask for. Keep on seeking, and you will find. Keep on knocking, and the door will be opened to you."

AUGUST 7

Champion,

Ask God to help you be a rejoicer, not a resenter, complainer or drainer. One produces life and the others produce death. One produces the muscle of perseverance, the mentality of hope, and the character of God. The other produces despair, depression and death. Keep the garment of praise on and you won't freeze to death in the cold circumstances of life.

Isaiah 61:3b "He will give a crown of beauty for ashes, a joyous blessing instead of mourning , festive praise instead of despair. In their righteousness, they will be like great oaks that the Lord has planted for His own glory."

Champion,

If evolution is true, then you are an accident. If God is the creator with a purpose in mind, then you are valuable, wanted, loved and have a very special purpose.

1 Peter 1:3 "All praise to God, the Father of our Lord Jesus Christ. It is by his great mercy that we have been born again, because God raised Jesus Christ from the dead. Now we live with great expectation,"

AUGUST 9

Champion,

The Lord says "I Am" the way and the truth that leads to abundant life there is no pleasure greater than that which is found in My presence. There is no greater Comforter than Me. Much love is waiting for you, draw near my friend, do not despise the Truth that will set you free. Ask God to help you value Him more than any of the man made little gods, that we can so easily put in first place before Him.

John 14:6 "Jesus told them" I am the way, the truth and the life. No one can come to the Father except through me"

Champion,

New thought Champion, "You do not work for a living." Every Christian is a missionary. We are the salt and the light of the earth. Salt preserves and makes things taste better. Light comforts and reveals, producing the answer. You are not called to work for a living. You are called instead, as an undercover agent representing the kingdom of God. So, you live to work. Because all the different jobs are really missionary fields, where people need to taste and see the goodness of God coming out of you. They need to learn how to rely on God and know that they are not alone. You work for Jesus and get paid by others. The shift in thinking makes life much more exciting. Your focus is on Jesus and what He is going to do through you. And the conversation at the dinner table is testimonials of what God did, instead of complaining about what others did or did not do.

Matthew 5:13a,16 "You are the salt of the earth. In the same way, let your good deeds shine out for all to see, so that everyone will praise your Heavenly Father."

Champion,

God is a PROMISE MAKER and PROMISE KEEPER. His promises are gifts that are unwrapped by faith. If you have any shred of doubt that God does not mean what He says, you will not boldly declare what He has promised. The tormenting giants will not fall , you will stay trapped, instead of free. What could have been, does not manifest. You will not live excited, you will not be filled with hope. Remember His nature, faithful. His integrity, truthful. He cannot lie, His ability, all powerful. Let the facts of His Nature IMPACT YOU! So, His promises empower you. STOP being intimidated by yours' and others' experiences. Ask God to deliver you from all that is hindering you from being fully alive and on fire with the FACTS of who HE IS. Ask Him to Fill You with His Promises and you will be Promise Empowered. Having strength, energy, courage, boldness, peace and joy like never before. STOP being bullied by the fear of disappointment. Take up the sword of the Spirit which is the word of God and declare who God is and what He has promised. So you can be and do what he has called you to become.

Numbers 23:19 "God is not a man, so He does not lie. He is not human, so He does not change His mind. Has He ever spoken and failed to act? Has He promised and not carried it through?"

Champion,

Valuable men and women, created by God. Spirit and soul health is the highest priority, without it there is no alignment with heaven and you will not fulfill your assignment. You have been preordained to do good works that manifest Heaven on earth. Jesus is the door that must be opened to receive the Breath of Heaven. That will empower you, renew your mind, and give you the spirit power that you do not have without relying on Jesus. You can live this life with or without batteries. Faith in Jesus provides the supernatural battery that can constantly be recharged by His presence and His word.

2 Timothy 3:16-17 "All scripture is inspired by God and is useful to teach us what is true and to make us realize what is wrong in our lives. It corrects us when we are wrong and teaches us to do what is right. God uses it to prepare and equip His people to do every good work."

Champion,

Whatever captures your heart and holds your attention controls your life!! God knows this and Satan knows this. Satan tried to capture the Heart of Jesus in the wilderness. In the wilderness of our personal journey the same voice that tempted Jesus speaks today and attempts to seduce us to go the wrong way. The easy way, instead of the right way. It's time to stand up and be counted and say like Jesus did "NO WAY!!" my Father is Yahweh. I will serve no other God. God Almighty created me!! God has a good plan for me!! And I will Fulfill My Destiny. By the Grace of God, and for the Glory of God. I will hear well done at the end of my journey!!!

1 Corinthians 10:13 "The temptations in your life are no different from what others experience. And God is faithful. He will not allow the temptation to be more than you can stand. When you are tempted, He will show you a way out so that you can endure."

Champion,

The fitness experts say that your core, the strength, quality or condition of your upper middle body, determines much about your health. They say the extra weight in the midsection is filled with toxins that deteriorate your body and cause much sickness . Also, the strength of your core can set you up for injury or victory. Even more important, according to God, is our core values, they effect every area of our life, on a daily basis. The Champions in the Bible that brought heaven to earth and helped people go from earth to heaven are known as Champions because their core value was "Honor God". No Matter The Cost. Let's Be Like Them and Rock The Nations!!!

1 Corinthians 6:19-20 "Don't you realize that your body is the temple of the Holy Spirit, who lives in you and was given to you by God? You do not belong to yourself, for God bought you with a high price. . So you must honor God with your body."

Champion,

An intimate relationship with the Father, through the door of Jesus, by the power of the Holy Spirit, is the greatest thing you'll ever experience. Constantly offer up your heart like a cup and ask Him to clean it and fill it, fill it and clean it. You will experience life on earth like none other. If you do not open your heart to the One that is knocking, you will be very sad later on. It is the most dynamic relationship available. Suggestion; hourly maintenance keeps you strong.

Revelation 3:20 "Look! I stand at the door and knock. If you hear My voice and open the door, I will come in, and we will share a meal together as friends."

Champion,

Follower of Christ, Jesus looked at them and said to them, "With man this is impossible, but with God all things are possible." The priest said to the army of Israel, "Do not be afraid! The Lord your God is going with you!" He will fight for you, against your enemies, and He will give you victory! If you are following, He will go before you and make a way where there is no way. You can expect miraculous help!!

Matthew 19:26 "Jesus looked at them intently and said, "Humanly speaking, it is impossible. But with God everything is possible"

Champion,

Psalm 149:4 The Lord takes pleasure in His people: He will beautify the humble with salvation. He will rescue, He will deliver, give aid, new victory, prosperity, health, help, saving health and adorn the wretched with victory. Amazing Grace, unmerited favor and His divine influence is still alive and well. The one that made us, can fix us. He will help us walk in humility and reverence for Him and you will experience life, honor and provision. Prov.22:4 ask Him to help you.

Proverbs 22:4 *"True humility and fear of the Lord lead to riches, honor, and long life."*

Champion,

FREEDOM -Get free from resentment that eats away at you and steals your strength and joy! A sign of true freedom is when you are able to whole-heartedly serve others in their passion instead of your own passion. When you value what other people value and serve them by doing things the way they want them done- you have matured. There is always a reward when we use God's wisdom. Jesus was the greatest servant of all. He did not come to earth to be served but to serve. (Matt. 20:28) Resentment is a fruit of jealousy. It's a deadly Virus that steals, kills and destroys. A true servant is the most blessed person on earth. Why? Because you are planting another seed that produces another harvest. Remember, everyone has specific servant assignments. Ask God to help you know and joyfully embrace the ones attached to your name!

John 8:36 "So if the Son sets you free, you are truly free."

Champion,

Be Encouraged!

God does not sleep nor slumber -He's awake working when you are sleeping. When you're sleeping He's watching you, thinking about you, caring for you. To prove that's true, this morning beginning at 3:30 a.m., He awakened me to pray for you-that you would experience the fullness of His goodness and manifest it; helping those around you taste and see His goodness. I prayed for the good plan He has for you. I prayed for you to be encouraged. God knows you- loves you- and has people praying for you. Remember, as a Follower of Christ, God promises that He will meet all your needs according to His riches in glory and will help you experience more than you can ask, think or imagine – that is what I prayed for and continue to pray for you...

Psalm 31:24 "Be strong and let your heart take courage, all you who wait for and hope for and expect the Lord!" (AMP)

Champion,

Ask God to help you be an expert at being grateful. Ask Him to heal your heart and renew your mind from anything and everything that would stop you from being grateful. Do this heart "work" and your home "will work". Take this prescription continually night and day and you will experience abundant life. Remember, what you look for you will find...If you set your heart on things to be thankful for and you will find them. This will produce rejoicing that increases strength vs. resentment that depletes your strength.

1 Thessalonians 5:18 "Be thankful in all circumstances, for this is God's will for you who belong to Christ Jesus."

August 21

Champion,

God has a good plan for You and a mighty hand to bring it to pass. Agree with Him- cooperate with Him -yield to Him and you will see it! Declare, "God has a good plan for me and I will see the fullness of His goodness by the Power of His Spirit!" Say it when it doesn't look like it's happening and you will be imitating Him who calls those things that are not as though they were. Do not back off -back down -slow down or stand down. Stand tall and speak in accordance with what God says. Do not talk about your mountains. Do not listen to the voice of your mountains...Speak!!!-Stand up to the bully that is tormenting you and say, " NO!!" " I will see the fullness of God's goodness that He has planned for me by the Grace of God for the Glory of God!"

Philippians 1:6 "And I am certain that God, who began a good work within you, will continue his work until it is finally finished on the day when Christ Jesus returns."

Champion,

If you want to Experience the Promised Land plan that God has for You- you are going to have to have a steady diet of Promise food and exercise. God's promises must be mixed with revelation and a constant proclamation, (no matter the circumstances), of His nature. Combine His promises with the revelation of His Nature and the weapon of faith will flow out of You like never before. Example: In Exodus 6:7, God brought His people out from under the yoke of the Egyptians. In Ex. 9:14-15, the Lord is faithful to His promises and delivers His people through His powerful right hand. In Ex. 15:17, God brought His people in and planted them on the mountain of His inheritance. My friends are you under a yoke? Do you need help? Do you need deliverance? Do you need to be brought out of something into something and planted in the new place that God has for you? Stand up and start thanking God that He is the same yesterday, today and forever. Ask Him and thank Him for complete deliverance of every yoke of bondage in your life so that you may be planted on the mountain of inheritance He has for you. Let's move our mountain of circumstances with words of faith and praise and declaration. Let's Influence the nations with God's Goodness!

Joshua 1:3 ..."Wherever you set foot, you will be on land I have given you."

Champion,

God is not a respecter of persons. Check out the story of the Centurion and he wasn't even a believer in Christ (Matt.. 8:5-13). The Spirit of God wants you to be charged with fresh Faith; that the goodness that others have experienced-the goodness of spiritual, mental, emotional, physical, financial and relational blessing can be yours. Be encouraged! Start thanking God for being amazing. Ask Him for forgiveness for any negativity or foolish talk about your problems and lift them all up to Him. Thank Him for new victory and don't ever stop no matter what you see. Faith does not operate by sight. It operates by the might that comes from understanding of who He is. Remember to feed your Heart on His promises and Celebrate what He has Already done for you! Be refreshed with...

Psalm 149:4 "For the Lord delights in His people; He crowns the humble with victory."

Champion,

Jesus said that He is the Bread of Life and Living Water. He said that those that hunger and thirst for righteousness will be satisfied. He said do not forsake the assembly of the Saints. There is bread and water waiting for you. There's a feeling of being satisfied waiting for you. There's a blessing from being part of an assembly waiting for you. Jesus said to His disciples, " Come, follow me." He is saying by His spirit to you today, "Come, follow me". Listen to His heart. You'll be glad you did!

Matthew 11:28 "Then Jesus said, Come, to me, all of you who are weary and have heavy burdens and I will give you rest."

Champion,

Look up! Drink in the truth...Soak your heart in the living reality of Jesus. As a Christian, you, too are God's treasured son or daughter. He does not look down on you. He will not condemn you or criticize you. He will never push you down, but reach down when you bow down they He may pull you up and out. When you don't feel valuable-remember Somebody greater than anybody LOVES YOU . Arise Out of the Fear of Man. Declare, "God is with me -God is for me-I will fear no evil – I will be controlled by One Spirit: The Holy Spirit!

Psalm 40:1-2 "He lifted me out of the pit of despair, out of the mud and mire. He set my feet on solid ground and steadied me as I walked along."

Champion,

Look for reasons to compliment, praise, encourage, edify and lift up. -Ask God to help you see the good.

Philippians 4:8 "Fix your thoughts on what is true, and honorable, and right, and pure, and lovely, and admirable."

Champion,

Our God is a Rewarder of those that diligently seek Him and follow Him. Do what is right in His Sight- and find goodness waiting for you. Lamentations 3:21-23 in Jeremiah says that it is because of the Lord's mercy and loving kindness that we are not consumed. It's because His tender compassion fails not. They are New Every Morning. Great and abundant is your stability and faithfulness God. The Lord is my portion, therefore I will hope in Him and wait expectantly for Him. The Lord is good to those who wait hopefully and expectantly in Him. Everywhere you look in the Bible there are promises for believing, for following, for surrendering to His leadership. Ask Him to help you so you don't miss out.

Proverbs 10:6 "The godly are showered with blessings..."

Champion,

Your Heartfelt earnest prayers avail much. God says what He means and means what He says. He is not a liar. He says not to add to or subtract anything from His Word, but many times we do when we don't understand our circumstances. Hold fast, my friend. Be steadfast. Press into His promises. Do not let His promises be pressed out of you! Increase your calorie intake of His promises and speak them out. Stop analyzing or apologizing and let His promises and His integrity cause a bonfire of faith inside of you. You cannot be strong in the Lord and the power of His might without the nutrients of His promises and the fiber of His integrity every day. Much love...

2 Samuel 22:31 "God's way is perfect. All the Lord's promises prove true. He is a shield for all who look to him for protection."

Champion,

Everywhere you look in the Bible. It's a Promise book from God! NOW mix faithfulness and truthfulness, (the integrity of God and the ability of God), with the promises and you have Promise Power resulting in Ferocious Fiery Faith! That's the equation my friend for unspeakable joy and peace that passes understanding. It will produce a Fearless Lifestyle. Soak your Heart in Psalm 23 and then make David's testimony your declaration. You will end up with the same testimony as David. God spoke and created, now you speak and create! That's how God's Kingdom first manifested in your Heart and that's how it continues to manifest around you.

James 2:17 "So you see, faith by itself isn't enough. Unless it produces good deeds, it is dead and useless."

Champion,

God's LOVE is not fickle, (unstable, unsteady), and it certainly does not trickle down from heaven. It is abundant. Draw near with your whole Heart and you will be Blessed !!

Ephesians 3:18 "And may you have the power to under-stand, as all God's people should, how wide, how long, how high, and how deep His love is."

August 31

Champion,

God is an ever-present help. All we have to do is believe and ask. He says ask for wisdom and He will give it to you liberally. He says that His tender mercies and loving kindness never fail and they are new every morning. You are in a war and your enemy wants you to stop believing. Never quit asking, pursuing or seeking. Asking Him is like a weapon. Don't put it down, no matter what! Stopping this strategy guarantees loss. He is faithful even when we are faithless.

Matthew 7:7 "Keep on asking you will receive what you ask for, keep on seeking, and you will find. Keep on knocking and the door will be opened to you."

Champion,

Whatever is coming out of your mouth is an indication of the health of your heart and the maturity of your mind. There are rules of engagement. Engaging your mouth and not paying attention to the rules will cause destruction: heartache for you and others. Beware when you don't speak truth in love, when your words are not seasoned with grace. When you slander, gossip, judge, complain or condemn others, you will reap what you sow. Go take a shower in God's presence and in His word and get cleaned up and cleaned out or you will miss out...

Proverbs 18:21 "The tongue can bring death or life; those who love to talk will reap the consequences."

Champion,

There is a place of amazing grace that supplies help in time of need. It is the throne of grace-where our Heavenly Father awaits. Come near...cry out...surrender in faith; you will not get an answering machine.

Jeremiah 33:3 "Ask me and I will tell you remarkable secrets you do not know about things to come."

Isaiah 30:21 "Your own ears will hear Him. Right behind you a voice will say, this is the way you should go."

Champion,

One prescription does it all-Leaning on the integrity and ability of our Heavenly Father and His Promises, because His favor is greater than any foolishness going on in your life. His Power, His Love, His Wisdom, His Goodness-they are all Greater. So be not afraid or discouraged! Rejoice in the fact that He is with you. Declare the truth out Loud-Shout it Out-and Stand!!

Ephesians 6:13 "Therefore, put on every piece of God's armor so you will be able to resist the enemy in the time of evil. Then after the battle you will still be standing firm."

Champion,

When you feel resent- Repent, (change your thinking). Resentment is the fruit of thoughts-the indicator that what you are thinking is stinking and you are sinking your own ship. Let go of the anger-anchor causing resentment. Ask God to help you be a rejoicer instead of a resenter and for His winning wisdom to help you overcome in every situation.

James 1:2-4 "Dear brothers and sisters, when trouble comes your way, consider it an opportunity for great joy. For you know that when your faith is tested, your endurance has a chance to grow. So let it grow, for when your endurance is fully developed, you will be perfect and complete, needing nothing."

Champion,

Serving the Lord, the supreme authority, the greatest leader of all time is rewarding, but not always easy. Sacrifice and the good fight of faith are part of the package. It is a mediocre man who wants the easy way out. Peace and Comfort are desired by all, but it is not produced by being passive. Peace is not the absence of war, but is the presence of God. Peace knows, He is with us in the battles of life. Fear of suffering causes passivity which causes greater suffering. God himself will remember, reward and honor those who give their lives, face their giants and confront fears. Those who fight bravely armed with His promises fulfill their destiny and finish their course.

2 Timothy 1:7 "For God has not given us a spirit of fear and timidity, but of power, love, and self-discipline."

SEPTEMBER 6

Champion,

I hear the Lord saying "it's time to be bold and come out of the old, arise and shine the Glory of the Lord is upon you and in you. Do not despise and surmise, but arise and say Lord help me come out of the old and into the new. So you can move in and through me like never before."

Acts 17:28 "For in Him we live and move and exist. As some of your own poets have said, 'We are his offspring'"

Champion,

Today, I hear the Lord saying "it's time to sow, grow and go," so you will grow like you never grown and go like you have never gone." God says "He gives seed to the sower," what seed is it? Wisdom, love, forgiveness, friendship, finances etc.) What does He want you to sow and where is He telling you to sow it? He can grow it, but if you do not sow it He cannot grow it. The Spirit of Fear keeps us from sowing , so we won't have the knowing, (the confidence), of God's amazing ability to multiply back to us what we have planted. A farmer never says "I have already done that." He looks for another field and plants the seed. Arise; do not despise the Wisdom of God and plant. Declare... "By the Grace of God, I sow everything that God wants me to sow and experience every harvest that He wants me to experience."

Leviticus 26:5 "Your threshing season will overlap with the grape harvest, and your grape harvest will overlap with the season of planting grain. You will eat your fill and live securely in your own land."

SEPTEMBER 8

Champion,

Correct Thinking Produces Great Results! Ask God to help you. Here is an example; I always have a reason to sing, to bring Praise to the King, and have a reason to Hope because of my God's faithfulness. His truthfulness, integrity, ability, and kindness always give me a reason to sing! Because of what He's already done, I always have a reason to sing. Ask Him to help you praise, it brings Heaven to earth!

Psalm 118:24 "This is the day the Lord has made. We will rejoice and be glad in it."

Champion,

Good News -The Lord takes pleasure in His people! He will beautify the humble with Salvation, (he will rescue, he will deliver, give aid, new victory, prosperity, health, help and saving health), and adorn the wretched with victory. Amazing Grace, (unmerited favor and His divine influence), is still alive and well. The one that made us can fix us and will help us walk in humility and reverence for Him and you will experience life, honor and provision. Ask Him to help you.

Psalm 149:4 "For the LORD takes delight in his people; he crowns the humble with victory." (NIV)

Proverbs 22:4 "Humility is the fear of the LORD; its wages are riches and honor and life." (NIV)

Champion,

Good News Champion –The God of all Creation thinks your Valuable, was crucified for you and lives for you! He is looking forward to hearing your heart, helping you, leading, guiding and filling you with His Power, love and wisdom. Enter the zone and stay in the zone by continually relying on Him. Praising Him constantly for what you already know about Him, talk to Him about everything and you will know Him like you have never known Him and there is nothing better.

Zephaniah 3:17 "For the LORD your God is living among you. He is a mighty savior. He will take delight in you with gladness. With his love, he will calm all your fears. He will rejoice over you with joyful songs." (NIV)

Champion,

Life is much easier when you embrace difficulties with rejoicing, not resenting. When you consider them an opportunity instead of a curse, not only will you decrease the suffering, but you'll see the breakthrough quicker. The very thing that Satan sent against you to destroy you will become the catalyst for God to make you into an overcomer not a be-moaner.

Revelation 12:11 "And they have defeated him by the blood of the Lamb and by their testimony. And they did not love their lives so much that they were afraid to die." (NIV)

September 12

Champion,

If you take a soaking bath in God's Promises, remembering the historical facts of His track record, that He is faithful, truthful and able, you will praise, pray and prophesy and move mountains in your life like you never have before. You will be a bulldozer empowered by His presence creating new roads that open up the way for you and others to experience God's goodness. The spirit of power, love and wisdom will flow out of you and destroy works of darkness like never before. Read the book of Psalms and be saturated with the reality of His amazing nature. Read a proverb a day and underline the promises of His wisdom. You will enter the day strong enabled to make a Good Day, instead of waiting to see if you're going to have a good day.

Micah 1:4 "The mountains melt beneath his feet and flow into the valleys like wax in a fire, like water pouring down a hill." (NIV)

Psalm 97:5 "The mountains melt like wax before the Lord, before the Lord of all the earth." (NIV)

Champion,

Rewards are waiting for you! God says "He is a rewarder of those that diligently pursue and follow Him." In the book of Matthew, Jesus said, "Go into a room and close the door and talk to the Heavenly Father and He will reward you publicly." In the book of Revelation God says "He will reward those that overcome." One of my favorites is Proverbs 22:4 "humility and reverence for God's wisdom produces life, honor and provision." Throughout the word of God it says be generous and you will be blessed. It also says if you have to leave something behind to follow Jesus you will be rewarded 100 fold in this lifetime. Psalm 23 says if the Lord is your shepherd and you are following Him, His goodness will pursue you and overtake you. So don't focus on what you see if it's the opposite. Focus on what He has said and His integrity. He is the "bring to pass, make away where there is no way" God! Let your heart and mind be saturated with these greater realities. Then stand up and declare what He has said and put fear to bed.

Revelation 3:21 "Those who are victorious will sit with me on my throne, just as I was victorious and sat with my Father on his throne."

Proverbs 22:4 "True humility and fear of the LORD lead to riches, honor, and long life."

SEPTEMBER 14

Champion,

The testimony of King David who knew God found in Psalm 16 speaking to God, he says, "you show me the path of life and in your presence there is fullness of joy; at your right hand are pleasures forevermore." So eat, drink and saturate your heart in the greater reality of who God is and His promises and you will thrive from the inside out. You will produce life with your mouth if you have life in your Heart.

Psalm 16:11 "You will show me the way of life, granting me the joy of your presence and the pleasures of living with you forever."

My friend,

If you ponder the reality of God's integrity and ability - you will not wander into the obscurity of insecurity and fear.

2 Timothy 1:7 "For God has not given us a spirit of fear and timidity, but of power, love, and self-discipline." (NIV)

Champion,

God's hand is not short, He is able to perform, and He makes a way where there is no way. Focus on what He has already done; stars, moon and sun with no strings attached mercy, forgiveness, His son and His spirit, water, food and air to breath. There is always a reason to praise Him. Do not let the grief of daily circumstances quench the greater reality of His goodness and destroy your Faith. Ask Him to help you stay clean and be strong through His wisdom of Healthy Heart Hygiene.

2 Samuel 22:33 "God is my strong fortress, and he makes my way perfect."

Isaiah 57:15 "The high and lofty one who lives in eternity, the Holy One, says this: "I live in the high and holy place with those whose spirits are contrite and humble. I restore the crushed spirit of the humble and revive the courage of those with repentant hearts."(NIV)

Champion,

Two Lifestyles: Proverbs 22:4-5 The Reward of Humility and the reverent and worshipful fear of the Lord is riches and honor and life, but thorns and snares are in the way of the obstinate and willful. He who humbles and trust God will not be caught in the thorns and snares of Life. Good News! We have the power to choose whether we live a life that produces rewards or consequences. Ask the Father to help you choose right. He will help you!

Proverbs 22:4-5 "Humility is the fear of the LORD; its wages are riches and honor and life. In the paths of the wicked are snares and pitfalls, but those who would preserve their life stay far from them." (NIV)

Champion,

One of the smartest things you could ever do is download the Promises of God into your Heart and Mix them with the reality of God's faithfulness, truthfulness and ability. Say No and resist the fear of disappointment that tries to stop you from believing. Believing produces hope, Joy, peace and a whole lot more of God's goodness.

James 4:7 "So humble yourselves before God. Resist the devil, and he will flee from you." (NIV)

Romans 14:17 "For the Kingdom of God is not a matter of what we eat or drink, but of living a life of goodness and peace and joy in the Holy Spirit." (NIV)

Champion,

The more you hang out with God and His people, the more of His wisdom and understanding you will get. The more encouraged, edified and empowered you will be and the more victory you will see, if you use what He gives you diligently.

Proverbs 1:7-9 "Fear of the LORD is the foundation of true knowledge, but fools despise wisdom and discipline. My child, listen when your father corrects you. Don't neglect your mother's instruction. What you learn from them will crown you with grace and be a chain of honor around your neck." (NIV)

Champion,

Whatever you magnify will control you Champion!! Psalm 70:4 May all those who seek, inquire of and for You, and require You as their vital need, rejoice and be glad in You; and may those who love Your salvation,healing,deliverance,freedom,joy,presence and victory say continually, "Let God be Magnified!" When you declare the promises of God and the nature of God, the Power of God is released to turn everything around and help you abound. So continue in faith and patience and you will reap a new testimony.

Psalm 70:4 "But may all who search for you be filled with joy and gladness in you. May those who love your salvation repeatedly shout, "God is great!"

Champion,

Loving people is not an event. Let's make it a 24/7 Lifestyle.

1 John 4:7-8 "Dear friends, let us continue to love one another, for love comes from God. Anyone who loves is a child of
God and knows God. But anyone who does not love does not
know God, for God is love."

Champion,

In Psalm 133, God says that He will command a blessing upon the unity of His people. He has promised that He will inhabit the praises of His people, Isaiah 57:15 declares : For thus says the One who is high and lifted up, who inhabits eternity, whose name is Holy: "I dwell in the high and holy place." Also with him who is of a humble and reverent spirit, to revive the spirit of the humble, and to revive the heart of the reverent one. 2 Chronicles 5:13-14 And when the trumpeters and singers were joined in unison, making one sound to be heard in praising and thanking the Lord, and when they lifted up their voice with the trumpets and cymbals and other instruments for song and praised the Lord, saying, "For He is good, for His mercy and loving kindness endure forever." Then the house of the Lord was filled with a cloud, so that the priests could not stand to minister because of the cloud, for the glory of the Lord filled the house of God.

Psalm 133 "How wonderful and pleasant it is when brothers live together in harmony! For harmony is as precious as the anointing oil that was poured over Aaron's head, that ran down his beard and onto the border of his. Robe. Harmony is as refreshing as the dew from Mount Hermon that falls on the mountains of Zion. And there the Lord has pronounced His blessing even life everlasting."

Champion,

James 1:12 Blessed are those who endure when they are tested, rejoicing instead of resenting, choosing life instead of death, choosing faith- instead of unbelief, peace instead of anxiety, humility, instead of pride. So when they pass the test of what they choose, they will receive the crown of life, that God has promised to those who love him, (hear and follow Him).Remember Champion, God, is a rewarder of those who diligently seek Him- Heb. 11:6.

James 1:12 "God blesses those who patiently endure testing and temptation. Afterward they will receive the crown of life that God has promised to those who love Him."

Champion,

Ask God to help you bless, give, and love like he does. You'll have more fun than ever! Look, listen and love.

Matthew 20:26-28 "But among you it will be different. Whoever wants to be a leader among you must be your servant, and whoever wants to be first among you must become your slave. For even the Son of Man came not to be a served but to serve others and to give His life as a ransom for many."

Champion,

Good morning, Again today I hear him say, COME! COME! COME! Draw near to the one that loves you more than anyone else.

Revelation 22:17 "The Spirit and the bride say, "Come." Let anyone who is thirsty come. Let anyone who desires drink freely from the water of life."

SEPTEMBER 26

Champion,

Don't run away from problems, run through them with your reliance and focus on Jesus. Because that's what he did. When hurt, anger and fear are trying to steer you the wrong way say; Help me Father! Help me Father! Help me Father! Remember Father means provider and He answers His calls. Faith and patience in Him produce results.

James 1:3-4 "For you know that when your faith is tested, your endurance has a chance to grow so let it grow, for when your endurance is fully developed, you will be perfect and complete, needing nothing."

Champion,

A Christian's number one goal should be to imitate and demonstrate the Father just like Jesus did. I pray that is a burning passion inside of you at all times getting better and better at it by the Power of his Spirit. Run that race and you will experience great fulfillment. Remember rely on Him.

John 5:19 "So Jesus explained, "I tell you the truth, the Son can do nothing by Himself. He does only what He sees the Father doing. Whatever the Father does, the Son also does."

Champion,

Gratefulness is the key to faithfulness and faithfulness is what the Father is looking for. Then you will flourish. When the Israelites stopped being grateful, they stopped being faithful, and they died prematurely. They resented the process to the promises. Their focus was on their present suffering, instead of their testimony of what God had done previously, So, instead of mixing faith with the un-comfortableness, they complained and drained the glory, instead of multiplying it through rejoicing. Ask God to help you live for his pleasure not yours and you will experience pleasure like none other.

Matthew 25:21 "The master was full of praise. 'Well done, my good and faithful servant. You have been faithful in the handling this small amount, so now I will give you many more responsibilities. Let's celebrate together!'

Champion,

Our Father has a good attitude. Having bad attitudes about things that God has a good attitude about causes us to despise and disdain something that he wants us to value. Be courageous and ask God what am I despising that I should be valuing? Actions not intentions, follow true valuing.

I John 5:14 "And we are confident that He hears us whenever we ask for anything that pleases Him."

Champion,

Yielding produces a field, Saying yes to what you know is right will produce a great harvest, if you do not give up. Following the Fathers Wisdom is the greatest thing you could ever do. Ask Him to help you and He will.

Galatians 6:9 "So let's not get tired of doing what is good. At just the right time we will reap a harvest of blessing if we don't give up."

Champion,

Somebody loves you ! Somebody wants you! Somebody has not rejected you! And He's greater than anyone else. Give Him your heart and He will fill it with new wisdom and love.

John 15:12-13 "This is my commandment: Love each other in the same way I have loved you. There is no greater love than to lay down one's life for one's friends."

Champion,

Good news! There is water in the pipes waiting to refresh you. All you have to do is turn on the handle of faith. Ask the Holy Spirit how does the Father want to refresh me this morning so I can imitate and demonstrate him today? Suggestion: remember who He is and what He has done for you and praise will spring out of you and you will be refreshed, if you stay in it long enough.

Revelation 2:16 "And He also said," It is finished! I am the Alpha and the Omega- the beginning and the end. To all who are thirsty I will give freely from the springs of the water of life."

Champion,

Every problem is temporary if your hope and actions are in the living, giving, Heavenly Father. Something good is about to happen. Think and say that truth and you will live above and not beneath.

Lamentations 3:14 "I say to myself, "The Lord is my inheritance; therefore, I will hope in Him!"

Champion,

When you want something, you pursue it. You find out the manufacturer and you find out where it is and you buy it. So it is with God. Peace, joy, and you want love. He has them all: wisdom, knowledge, understanding. They're all available. The price? Teachableness, time and practicing His strategies. Ask Him to help you and you will taste and see his goodness. Then experience the greatest joy; giving it out!

Psalms 34:8 "Taste and see that the Lord is good. Oh, the joys of those who take refuge in Him!"

Champion,

Be quick to pray and slow to say and you will slay every strategy of Satan coming through people. Remember, people are not the problem! It's principalities and powers working to destroy them and you. Pray! Pray! Pray! Do not let a fiery dart of offense stay in you. Immediately use the antidote for the snakebite; Pray, help me Father, help me Father, help me Father, help him Father, help them Father, help them Father. Use this and you will destroy mountains instead of create them with your mouth.

Proverbs 18:21 "The tongue can bring death or life; those who love to talk will reap the consequences."

Champion,

Jesus said, Traditions of men stop the power of God. Consider what traditions are stopping you; fear of man, what other people think, political correctness, what? Denial, fear of suffering, staying hurt instead of doing something about it. Be courageous and ask the Father what traditions of man, something this culture says is okay. What are you operating in that is stopping his power? Keeping his goodness from manifesting in your life? Pursue the truth and use it and you'll be set free.

Mark 7:13 "And so you cancel the word of God in order to hand down your own tradition. And this is only one example among many others."

Champion,

Jesus said he would send the Holy Spirit. Another Comforter. He said that if you saw Jesus, you saw the Father so the whole nature of God; Father, Son and Holy Spirit is Comforter. Pursue Him in your time of need and you will know the reality of his ability, and confidence and courage will permeate you. Experience real life today and every day, instead of the bondage that the other comforters bring.

John 14:26 "But when the Father sends the Advocate as my representative—that is, the Holy Spirit—he will teach you everything and will remind you of everything I have told you."

Champion,

Jesus told the religious leaders that they were good at cleaning the outside of the cup but not the inside. It's the condition of your heart that's most important. It affects every area of your life. It's the difference between being fully alive or half dead. Get alone with the one that loves you more than anyone else and ask Him to clean out all the toxins in your heart. You will live longer and laugh louder, make it your highest priority, consistent habit and you will know a life like none other. It is the plague of disappointments that destroys more than anything else.

Luke 11:39 "Then the Lord said to him, " You Pharisees are so careful to clean the outside of the cup and the dish, but inside you are filthy--full of greed and wickedness!"

Champion,

The snakebites of disappointments need the antidote of God's wisdom IMMEDIATELY or they will paralyze you! Hurt hinders and denying it is stupid. Do not pendulum! Retaliation does not work and saying you do not care does not work. Be honest; say to the Father, "that really hurt, I need help, please heal my heart. I choose forgiveness and I pray for that person, I bless them." This is the prescription that will keep you free and fully alive.

Proverbs 3:14-15 "For wisdom is more profitable than silver, and her wages are better than gold. Wisdom is more precious than rubies; nothing you desire can compare with her."

Champion,

When you turn on the praise, the rain begins and the refreshing is released. New life, new strength, new peace, new wisdom, new clarity, new confidence in the One that loves you more than anyone else. He accepts you and wants you!

Psalm 22:26b "All who seek the Lord will praise Him, their hearts will rejoice with everlasting joy!"

Champion,

The Lord says on this day, if you stick around, the waves of His goodness will abound. When you feel like you are sinking in the sand where he told you to stand, be not afraid. Continue to praise and give thanks and declare: "the Lord is my shepherd!" The waves of His goodness will come and you will find yourself riding high instead of sinking low.

Psalm 23:1-3 "The LORD is my shepherd; I have all that I need. He lets me rest in green meadows; he leads me beside peaceful streams. He renews my strength. He guides me along right paths, bringing honor to his name."

Champion,

Find a private place and shut the door and start thanking the Father and Jesus. Give them praise telling them how much you appreciate them and you will experience the more that is waiting for you. This cannot happen without using and following His divine strategies. Do not be satisfied with the worldly blessings when the greatest blessing, the supernatural presence of the one that loves you more than anybody else is waiting for you.

Matthew 6:6 "But when you pray, go away by yourself, shut the door behind you, and pray to your Father in private. Then your Father, who sees everything, will reward you."

Champion,

Declare the word of God. If you meditate and speak out loud Psalm 91 you will be energized and strengthened. The following instruction from Apostle Paul will be easy and you will be blessed and be a blessing. Hebrews 13: 15 & 16 Through Him, therefore, let us Constantly and at All times offer up to God a sacrifice of praise, which is the fruit of lips that thankfully acknowledge and confess and Glorify His name. Do not forget or neglect to do kindness and good.

Hebrews 13:15&16 "Therefore, let us offer through Jesus a continual sacrifice of praise to God, proclaiming our allegiance to his name. And don't forget to do good and to share with those in need. These are the sacrifices that please God."

Champion,

The Lord says "Change is the answer, if you want change" and it begins with you! It always begins on the inside of a person, how they think and what they are saying. The Lord said to Joshua if you think and say the word of the Lord, you will have good success. Example: if you want more peace, change your meditation. God says those that set their mind on Him and put their affections on Him will have perfect peace. So ask God to help you think about His faithfulness throughout history. He has always followed through on what He said He was going to do. So soak your heart in Psalm 91 and be empowered to think differently and speak supernaturally according to what God has said in Psalm 91.

Isaiah 26:3 "You will keep in perfect peace all who trust in you, all whose thoughts are fixed on you." (NIV)

Champion,

Stand up and Prophesy like Ezekiel did in chapter 37 My Friend. Speak to everything dry and dead in your life. Everything that is not working properly and declare that the Lord is your Shepard and you dwell in the secret place of the most high and you will experience every bit of goodness that God has for you and be Blessed and be a Blessing in every way that God has ordained you to be because of His integrity, willingness and ability. Be content Champion, but do not be a settler. Ask God to help you be 10 times better, like Daniel and 1000 times greater, like Moses. So the nations are rocked and taste and see the goodness of God. Pick up the sword of the spirit, which is the word of God, and declare Psalm 91 and you will experience some real fun, freedom, joy, peace and wisdom that nothing else can produce.

Ezekiel 37:1-4 "The LORD took hold of me, and I was carried away by the Spirit of the LORD to a valley filled with bones. 2 He led me all around among the bones that covered the valley floor. They were scattered everywhere across the ground and were completely dried out. 3 Then he asked me, "Son of man, can these bones become living people again?" "O Sovereign LORD," I replied, "you alone know the answer to that." 4 Then he said to me, "Speak a prophetic message to these bones and say, 'Dry bones, listen to the word of the LORD! 5 This is what the Sovereign LORD says: Look! I am going to put breath into you and make you live again! 6 I will put flesh and muscles on you and cover you with skin. I will put breath into you, and you will come to life. Then you will know that I am the LORD. "

Champion,

Psalm 34:8-10 This humble man cried, and the Lord heard him, and saved him out of all his troubles. The Angel of the Lord encamps around those who fear Him who revere and worship Him with awe and each of them He delivers. O taste and see that the Lord our God is good! Blessed happy, fortunate, to be envied is the man who trusts and takes refuge in Him. O fear the Lord, you His saints revere and worship Him! For there is no want to those who truly revere and worship Him with Godly fear. The young lions lack food and suffer hunger, but they who seek, inquire of and require the Lord by right of their need and on the authority of His Word, none of them shall lack any beneficial thing. NO BENEFICIAL THING- BAM!! Let these promises and those of Psalm 91 saturate your heart and ignite a confession of faith that moves every mountain. Speak the promises not the problems!! You are NOT a victim. Arise the glory of the Lord is in you and on you. You are a victor do not back down no matter what you see continue to speak accordingly no matter what.

Psalm 34:8-10 "Taste and see that the LORD is good. Oh, the joys of those who take refuge in him! Fear the LORD, you his godly people, for those who fear him will have all they need. Even strong young lions sometimes go hungry, but those who trust in the LORD will lack no good thing."

My Friend,

Be not intimidated, champion of Almighty God. Stand up and prophesy the word of the Lord and every mountain of obstacles will be turned into a molehill, even a plain. Stand up and declare Psalm 91, Psalm 23 & Jeremiah 29:11 and see and sense the power of God being released on your behalf.

Zechariah 4:7 'What are you, O great mountain [of obstacles]? Before Zerubbabel [who will rebuild the temple] you will become a plain (insignificant)! And he will bring out the capstone [of the new temple] with loud shouts of "Grace, grace to it!" (AMP)

OCTOBER 18

Champion,

Taste and know the goodness of God seek Him and you'll find Him. Love and wisdom come from and are the very nature of the same God. Love without wisdom is not good and wisdom without love is not good. Ask the Father to give you an abundance of both because we are accountable for what we think, say and do. Be quick to listen and slow to speak.

Psalm 34:8 "Taste and see that the Lord is good. Oh, the joys of those who take refuge in him!"

Champion,

The Lord says "do not be pulled out of your position or change your decision." His grace will make a place and enable you to run the race that He has called you to. Declare on this 19th day: "the Lord is my Shepherd and provision is not a problem. He will make away every single day for me to be and do His good plan."

Hebrews 12:1 "Therefore, since we are surrounded by such a huge crowd of witnesses to the life of faith, let us strip off every weight that slows us down, especially the sin that so easily trips us up. And let us run with endurance the race God has set before us."

OCTOBER 20

Champion,

There is only one door that leads to your Amazing Destiny. Put your hand on the knob and turn the handle on this 20th day by declaring the "The Lord is my shepherd" consistently, constantly and do not stop no matter what you see and you will experience the more than before and be strengthened, refreshed, under-girded and sustained.

John 14:6 "Jesus told him, "I am the way, the truth, and the life. No one can come to the Father except through me." (NIV)

Champion,

When life becomes about who loves you more than anyone else, (the Heavenly Father, Jesus and Holy Spirit) and what He has already done for you and not about what you like or don't like, then you will not be an emotional roller coaster up and down and all around no matter the circumstances. You will be found rejoicing because this is the day that the Lord has made. Honoring Him will be your first priority, hearing and doing His word will be a constant joy, and peace will not be a part time reality, but a full-time experience.

Psalm 118:24 "This is the day the Lord has made. We will rejoice and be glad in it."

Champion,

The Lord wants to remind you, the only thing that will ruin your day is Fear. Worse thing you could do is say yes to fear and mix fear producing thoughts with any problem or situation. Ask God to help you not to be afraid, but be very sober that you need Him more than anything else and that following Him and experiencing Him is what causes abundant life. So soak your heart in His word eat and drink Psalm 91 and declare it out of your mouth. What you say makes a way or blocks the way for more of His goodness. He is watching over the words of our mouth to bring them to pass according to His goodwill.

Romans 12:2 "Don't copy the behavior and customs of this world, but let God transform you into a new person by changing the way you think. Then you will learn to know God's will for you, which is good and pleasing and perfect."

Champion,

If you do the Kingdom thing you will see the Kingdom come. Exercise your faith muscle and say what God has said or is saying not what you see. Today He said- "I bring my people out of darkness into light, out of the tight space into the spacious place. The things you've been dealing with for years, months and weeks I will cause deliverance in days, hours and seconds. I will give you beauty for ashes. I will give you double for all your troubles. Arise and despise what you see and say what I say. STOP being bullied by the fear of disappointment. Stop allowing my Spirit to be quenched and your spirit immobilized. Stir up My Spirit that is within you and for you and declare: God's goodness will manifest in me, through me and all around me and I will be blessed and be a blessing and fulfill my destiny."

1 Peter 2:9 "But you are not like that, for you are a chosen people. You are royal priests, a holy nation, God's very own possession. As a result, you can show others the goodness of God, for he called you out of the darkness into his wonderful light."

Champion,

From Disappointment to Delight. That's what happens when you spend private time in a private place, bringing your heart to Jesus and our Father first thing in the morning. Oh the secret place of His presence nothing compares He is available 24 /7. The fruit of Psalm 91 can be yours, read and declare.

Matthew 6:6 "But when you pray, go away by yourself, shut the door behind you, and pray to your Father in private. Then your Father, who sees everything, will reward you."

Champion,

The only thing that will quench your thirst is Jesus, His voice and His presence through His Words and Spirit. It's the only thing that promises fullness of Joy. If you seek you will find. Find a private place and you will experience His amazing grace.

Isaiah 44:3 "For I will pour out water to quench your thirst and to irrigate your parched fields. And I will pour out my Spirit on your descendants, and my blessing on your children."

Champion,

Until you leave your comfort zone like Jesus did and live for others you will never experience resurrection life and produce the testimony that makes a way for others, which is the greatest thrill of all. Pick up your cross and follow me means leave your comfort zone, deny yourself and focus on being a blessing. Loving others and preferring others that's the way to true honor and supernatural provision because you reap what you sow. Do it because it is the way of wisdom, but know that if the harvest does not come quickly it's because your heart is being purified. When you are willing to do the right thing no matter when you see the harvest, that's perfect love. Your highest priority is honoring the Father and you are living to bring him the pleasure of seeing you walk by faith, choosing life, imitating Him, loving others, preferring others and serving others no matter what.

Luke 9:23 "Then he said to the crowd, "If any of you wants to be my follower, you must turn from your selfish ways, take up your cross daily, and follow me."

Champion,

If life is not about you, if it's about being a blessing to the Father and other people, you will never be offended. You will never be bound in judgments you could make of other people or even God himself. You won't become disconnected from the greatest life source of all, Jesus and His body. You will also hear the Heavenly Father say "well done! You have overcome."

Romans 12:9 "Don't just pretend to love others. Really love them. Hate what is wrong. Hold tightly to what is good."

Champion,

"Have to's" are desires with a fire that consumes excuses and compromise and making you the Champion that you are called to be. "Have to's" come from "experiencing something" and are usually fueled by the continuance of that "something". A "have to" attitude locks on and does not let go. The Holy Spirit is constantly at work to create "have to" desires with that consuming fire inside of you, so that you experience the fullness of God's good plan. Then the full nature of Jesus is coming out of you and people taste and see the goodness of God. "Have to's", created by the work of the Holy Spirit, create priorities and habits that lead to abundant life. Here are some of them..."I have to honor The Heart of God". "I have to love Him and people the way He wants me to." "I have to hear His voice and follow it." "I have to experience His presence daily and receive new grace so I can do His goodwill and pleasure." "I have to eat and drink His word and cooperate with His spirit." If you recognize that your "have to's" are something different, ask The Father to help you. He already wants to and will do it without condemning you.

Psalm 42:1-2 "As the deer longs for streams of water, so I long for you, O God. I thirst for God, the living God. When can I go and stand before him?"

Champion,

Good News – there is a way to be happy that produces abundant life instead of bondage. Proverbs 8:32-36 Now therefore listen to me, O you sons; for blessed happy, fortunate, to be envied are those who keep my (wisdom) ways. Hear instruction and be wise, and do not refuse or neglect it. Blessed happy, fortunate, to be envied is the man who listens to me, watching daily at my gates, waiting at the posts of my doors. For whoever finds me (Wisdom) finds life and draws forth and obtains favor from the Lord. But he who misses me or sins against me wrongs and injures himself; all who hate me (wisdom) love and court death. James 1:5 If any of you is deficient in wisdom, let him ask of the giving God who gives to everyone liberally and un-grudgingly, without reproaching or faultfinding, and it will be given him. Equation for Happy: draw near with an attitude of gratitude, thanking Him for the invitation to know Him and hear Him. Then by faith ask for wisdom and believe He Will give it to you. Ask Him to help you recognize it when He does and receive it then you will be Happy when you use it and find out it works.

James 1:5 "If you need wisdom, ask our generous God, and he will give it to you. He will not rebuke you for asking."

Champion,

Like Jesus, giving causes gain. That's why it's more blessed to give than receive. If you hoard you will be bored, if you hold back you will experience lack. Give praise constantly to the Father and those around you. Ask the Father to bless you so you can be a blessing. Ask the Father to help you be a full-time giver of what He has given you. It's the best way to live.

Matthew 6:3 "But when you give to someone in need, don't let your left hand know what your right hand is doing."

Champion,

For behavior to change, yours or others, the mind must be renewed into correct thinking and the heart must be healed from wounding of the past. Ask the Father for complete transformation to happen for you and others. Prayer is the most important step.

Colossians 1:13,14 "For he has rescued us from the kingdom of darkness and transferred us into the Kingdom of his dear Son, Who purchased our freedom and forgave our sins."

Champion,

Psalm 23 translates to the goodness of God pursues and over-takes those that walk in humility and reverence for the Heavenly Father, and His wisdom is Leadership. When it does not look like it, Romans 8:28 says don't be moved by what you see, continue to believe and confess.

Romans 8:28 "And we know that God causes everything to work together for the good of those who love God and are called according to his purpose for them."

Champion,

God made you, your good, Jesus died for you, you are valuable and the Holy Spirit lives inside of you. You are naturally supernatural, say no to that slimy stinky spirit of fear that is always trying to control us. Confess Jeremiah 29:11 "My Heavenly Father has a great hope and future for me and because of his truthfulness his faithfulness and his ability I can have joy today." What you believe and speak creates your world. Decorate your future with it today and forever.

Jeremiah 29:11 "For I know the plans I have for you," says the LORD. "They are plans for good and not for disaster, to give you a future and a hope."

Champion,

Fill your heart with heavenly paint and you will create heavenly colors with your mouth. Fill your heart with divine wisdom and create your world with divine exhortation refined just for you. When you are hurt and angry, STOP! and separate yourself and ask the Father to cleanse your heart of the frustration and fill it with new wisdom, new love and new peace. If you don't you will cause MORE pain for yourself and others.

Isaiah 57:15 "The high and lofty one who lives in eternity, the Holy One, says this: "I live in the high and holy place with those whose spirits are contrite and humble. I restore the crushed spirit of the humble and revive the courage of those with repentant hearts."

Champion,

When people don't do what you want them to do, ask God to help you not be mad, offended and/or judgmental. Don't say I don't care, say my Heavenly Father provides for me and He will make away for me to know the goodness He has for me.

Isaiah 43:19 "For I am about to do something new. See, I have already begun! Do you not see it? I will make a pathway through the wilderness. I will create rivers in the dry wasteland."

Champion,

Fear of suffering is the number one reason people are afraid and some sort of suffering is the reason they are angry. So unconsciously we seek pleasure and comfort as our main priority. So that means we may resist any Godly wisdom that may threaten our pleasure or comfort. Mature love is following the Father's wisdom and leadership, whether it's comfortable, inconvenient or there is a possibility of suffering. There is only one place of true freedom; true love and full-time worship, bowing down to nothing but Him. So ask God to help you not to be anxious because there's nothing he can't turn around. He can produce some kind of blessing out of anything. You will always receive greater rewards, greater pleasure and greater comfort following His wisdom.

Proverbs 1:7 "Fear of the LORD is the foundation of true knowledge, but fools despise wisdom and discipline."

Champion,

Agree with God this morning; you are loved, wanted and accepted, because of what Jesus did and His goodness pursues you and overtakes you. Let that fill your heart and flow out of your mouth and miracles will manifest. When it looks like they are not, don't back down, stand-down or slowdown stay in agreement and decree the words of life.

3 John 1:2 "Dear friend, I hope all is well with you and that you are as healthy in body as you are strong in spirit."

Champion,

The Father says that His ways and His thoughts are higher than ours. Ask Him to fill you with his higher thoughts, so you can do his higher ways and watch the difference it makes. You will have a testimony. I guarantee it.

Isaiah 55:9 "For just as the heavens are higher than the earth, so my ways are higher than your ways and my thoughts higher than your thoughts."

Champion,

To experience abundant life your heart needs consistent cleansing and refilling of new Love and wisdom that you get from intimacy with the Father. Jesus said if you spend time alone behind a closed door pursuing the heart of God you would be rewarded in public by the Father.

Psalm 51:10 "Create in me a clean heart, O God. Renew a loyal spirit within me."

Champion,

To experience abundant life you must when making a decision, stop and ask yourself, "Am I making this decision for comfort sake, because it's comfortable or because I'm following the leadership of the comforter, the Holy Spirit?" Are you serving the god of comfort or the One that leads you through the uncomfortable zone into new victory and testimony of His faithfulness? Your future depends on it. Be very alert!

Deuteronomy 30:19 & 20 "Today I have given you the choice between life and death, between blessings and curses. Now I call on heaven and earth to witness the choice you make. Oh, that you would choose life, so that you and your descendants might live! You can make this choice by loving the Lord your God, obeying him, and committing yourself firmly to him. This is the key to your life. And if you love and obey the Lord, you will live long in the land the Lord swore to give your ancestors Abraham, Isaac, and Jacob."

Champion,

We are either focused on the wounds of Jesus and walk in a revelation of His goodness or the wounds of people and focus on badness. The first one produces peace and life the second fear and anxiety.

1 Peter 2:9 "But you are not like that, for you are a chosen people. You are royal priests, a holy nation, God's very own possession. As a result, you can show others the goodness of God, for he called you out of the darkness into his wonderful light."

NOVEMBER 11

Champion,

When your focus is on God's goodness and not on people's badness, you will continue to praise and be constantly refreshed and fear and anger will not control you. Every problem is a package, read the label. Do not mix fear, anger, resentment, cursing, complaining or self-pity with what's in the package there will be harmful results. Ask God to help you be a problem shrinker, not a problem maximizer.

Philippians 4:8 "And now, dear brothers and sisters, one final thing. Fix your thoughts on what is true, and honorable, and right, and pure, and lovely, and admirable. Think about things that are excellent and worthy of praise."

Champion,

Recognize the "I don't want to" attitude and get rid of "I can't" from your daily vocabulary. Let's be honest, it usually means "I'm afraid" or "I would rather have somebody else do it for me." This is childish and lazy. It's better and more expedient to say "He can, and, I will do the right thing by the power of God within me." You will experience new energy and accomplish so much more good and in the end you will hear well done my good and faithful one.

Matthew 25:21 "The master was full of praise. 'Well done, my good and faithful servant. You have been faithful in handling this small amount, so now I will give you many more responsibilities. Let's celebrate together!"

Champion,

If you said yes to Jesus, you are a Son of God, you have favor with God and you have an advantage. If you would be faithful to thank Him for what you have already received and continue to believe that the favor of God is with you, no matter what you see, you will have and maintain peace and you will experience even more favor.

Matthew 5:9 "Blessed [spiritually calm with life-joy in God's favor] are the makers and maintainers of peace, for they will [express His character and] be called the sons of God." (AMP)

Champion,

The Lord says put your Hope in my integrity instead of the lottery. Continue to honor me and you will see the totality of what I have promised. Your needs will be met beyond what you could think, ask or imagine and I will even give you the desires of your heart if your heart stays soft towards me. I am not kidding, says the Lord, remain true and I will produce the breakthrough.

Psalm 25:5 "Lead me by your truth and teach me, for you are the God who saves me. All day long I put my hope in you."

My Friend,

Please hear the heart of God. He wants to bless you. The Lord just said, "There are things that I want to give My kids, My people, but I can't because they're not following my instructions. They are not receiving the corrections. They are not making the adjustments or asking me to help them make the adjustments. They are not taking responsibility for themselves, just making excuses. They are not repenting, and repentance always opens the door for the Kingdom of God to manifest, for the King to walk in, and for the goodness of God to manifest." If this word is for you, cry out for help. His mercy is new every morning. If you think it's for somebody you know, imitate The Heavenly Father and be compassionate and cry out on their behalf.

Proverbs 10:17 "People who accept discipline are on the pathway to life, but those who ignore correction will go astray."

Champion,

Joy comes in the morning when you remember how much you are loved by the Heavenly Father and Jesus, and realize and remember His mercies are new every morning. Take a few minutes, or many, and thank and praise Him for that and you will taste and see the goodness of the secret place -of His amazing presence.

Psalm 34:8 "Taste and see that the LORD is good. Oh, the joys of those who take refuge in him!"

Champion,

Good news! You can be happy instead of hopeless because you are not helpless. There is NEVER a reason to be hopeless. That is deception because God, the Heavenly Father, is alive and available through faith in Jesus and no one loves you more, and wants to help you more, than Him. All you have to do is choose life. Choose Him!

Psalm 25:5 "Lead me by your truth and teach me, for you are the God who saves me. All day long I put my hope in you."

Champion,

Exercise your faith in Him. Do not let any circumstance, disappointment, or hurt cause you to be lazy and forsake the resource center of abundant life--His word and presence, and local assembly. He never called you to live in a house of hopelessness, disappointment, discouragement, and upset that makes you bitter, angry, isolated, alone, and afraid. Seek and you will find all the ingredients needed to heal your heart, change your attitude and outlook, and be strong and unafraid.

Proverbs 3:13-18 "Happy -Blessed, fortunate, enviable is the man who finds skillful and godly wisdom, and the man who gets understanding drawing it forth from God's Word and life's experiences, for the gaining of it is better than the gaining of silver, and the profit of it better than fine gold."

Champion,

Over the next 21 days, read Proverbs 1 through 21 in addition to your Champions devotion today. Read and pray, (ask God to help you apply the instructions), and Declare, (what you are reading and praying about), that you will be and do by the Grace of God and bring Glory to God and experience the promises of using His word.

Proverbs 1:7 "Fear of the Lord is the foundation of true knowledge, but fools despise wisdom and discipline."

Champion,

Isaiah 41:10 says, "So do not fear, for I am with you; do not be dismayed, for I am your God. I will strengthen you and help you; I will uphold you with my righteous right hand." This is a promise to all those that put their hope and faith in Jesus and follow Him as their shepherd leader - provider.

Deuteronomy 31:6 "So be strong and courageous! Do not be afraid and do not panic before them. For the LORD your God will personally go ahead of you. He will neither fail you nor abandon you."

Gratitude Champion,

Preparing for Thanksgiving remember that gratitude will bring your joy level to a whole new latitude and impact for the good of everyone. Look for the good and lift up the "bad and sad" to God. Practice gratitude. You'll experience new life, a new love and a new strength.

Ps. 138:1-31 "Give you thanks, O Lord, with all my heart; I will sing your praises before the gods. I bow before your holy Temple as I worship. I praise your name for your unfailing love and faithfulness; for your promises are backed by all the honor of your name. As soon as I pray, you answer me; you encourage me by giving me strength."

Champion,

When you praise, compliment and give thanks you are honoring and loving, lifting and inspiring and encouraging and empowering. Ask God to help you do it with sincerity and pure genuineness. By the way, when you're complaining, criticizing and condemning you're draining, destroying and killing. Ask God to deliver you from the root causes of that behavior. It's a deadly virus.

John 10:10 "The thief's purpose is to steal and kill and destroy. My purpose is to give them a rich and satisfying life." (NIV)

Champion,

Ask God to Help you be an expert at Being Grateful. Champion ask Him to heal your heart and renew your mind from anything and everything that would stop you from being grateful. Do your homework by soaking your heart in His truths at your home and work. Stop and take these prescriptions and you will experience abundant life.

Philippians 4:6,7 "Don't worry about anything; instead, pray about everything. Tell God what you need, and thank him for all he has done. Then you will experience God's peace, which exceeds anything we can understand. His peace will guard your hearts and minds as you live in Christ Jesus." (NIV)

Champion,

Gratitude gets God's Attention - He responds with more goodness to thankfulness, it opens the Gates of Heaven and allows you intimate access to God. Do not despise the small, look for reasons to be grateful you will find them.

Psalm 138:1-3 "I give you thanks, O LORD, with all my heart; I will sing your praises before the gods. I bow before your holy Temple as I worship. I praise your name for your unfailing love and faithfulness; for your promises are backed by all the honor of your name. As soon as I pray, you answer me; you encourage me by giving me strength." (NIV)

Champion,

If blessing and serving others is your focus Champion, then you are in alignment with Heaven. Jesus said whatever you do for the least of them, you have done it for Him. Jesus said loving others is like loving Him. Live for others and consider yourself that you are Born to bless, Live to give and Love to Serve the Heart of the Heavenly Father. You will experience no greater joy, no greater life. Ask Him for the wisdom and the strength to do it.

Matthew 25:45 "And he will answer, 'I tell you the truth, when you refused to help the least of these my brothers and sisters, you were refusing to help me."(NIV)

Champion,

As soon as you feel irritated about something pray right away. Pursue peace, then and only then, with peace in your heart, you will know what to do next.

Philippians 4:7 "Then you will experience God's peace, which exceeds anything we can understand. His peace will guard your hearts and minds as you live in Christ Jesus."

Psalm Therapy -

For the next several days we will learn how to be "Blessed, Happy and Fortunate." Wisdom-when you read it thank God for His wisdom and for His desire for you to be blessed and His willingness to empower you to be a blessing. There is no greater thrill. Then turn it into a Declaration, like this;"By the Grace of God for the Glory of God I am a blessed, happy, fortunate, enviable person because..."

Psalm 1:1-3 "Blessed happy, fortunate, prosperous, and enviable is the man who walks and lives not in the counsel of the ungodly following their advice, their plans and purposes, nor stands submissive and inactive in the path where sinners walk, nor sits down to relax and rest where the scornful and the mockers gather. But his delight and desire are in the Wisdom of the Lord, and on His Principles- the precepts, the instructions, the teachings of God he habitually meditates ponders and studies by day and by night. And he shall be like a tree firmly planted and tended by the streams of water, ready to bring forth its fruit in its season; its leaf also shall not fade or wither; and everything he does shall prosper and come to maturity."

Psalm Therapy -

What You Magnify, Multiplies. What you magnify causes a manifestation. You can always tell what a person is meditating on (what they're thinking on) by their behavior. Psalm 2:12 "O blessed happy, fortunate, and to be envied are all those who seek refuge and put their trust in Him!" If you are truly trusting God, you will be found constantly Magnifying His identity, His integrity, His ability and His promises. You will be found declaring these things, and by doing so, peace, strength and wisdom will multiply and you will experience His presence and His power. When you magnify the reality of who God is instead of magnifying the problems. You will have peace instead of fear, rejoicing instead of resentment, Joy instead of depression, strength instead of weakness. Whatever you meditate on is what you're magnifying and what you're magnifying on creates a manifestation. Use this principal in every area-magnify the good by meditating on the good and looking for the good, you will have good results. You'll have Power, love, wisdom and strength to deal with the bad. The pain and the fear of the bad shrinks when you meditate on the good.

Psalm Therapy -

Psalm 40:4 "Blessed happy, fortunate, to be envied is the man who makes the Lord his refuge and trust, and turns not to the proud or to followers of false gods." The Lord says when you feel the pressure increase your praise and like Apostle Paul the doors that have you locked in and locked up will blow open. He said yesterday "do not allow your praise to be held hostage by circumstances." He said if you "increase your praise you will have peace instead of panic." No need to run away Champion-no need to be afraid or dismayed- if you remember who your God is you will be found praising instead of panicking. Release what you're holding and start Beholding- ME, says the Lord -I am the way the truth and the life. If you do -you will experience promotion in the midst of commotion because people are looking for pillars of peace, an oasis to run to. Psalm 18:28 "You, Lord, keep my lamp burning; my God turns my darkness into light."

Psalm Therapy -

Psalm 32:1-8 "Blessed happy, fortunate, to be envied is he who has forgiveness of his transgression continually exercised upon him, whose sin is covered. Blessed happy, fortunate, to be envied is the man to whom the Lord imputes no iniquity and in whose spirit there is no deceit. When I kept silence before I confessed, my bones wasted away through my groaning all the day long. For day and night Your hand of displeasure was heavy upon me; my moisture was turned into the drought of summer. I acknowledged my sin to You, and my iniquity I did not hide. I said, I will confess my transgressions to the Lord continually unfolding the past till all is told—then You instantly forgave me the guilt and iniquity of my sin. For this forgiveness let everyone who is godly pray—You are a hiding place for me; You, Lord, preserve me from trouble, You surround me with songs and shouts of deliverance. I the Lord will instruct you and teach you in the way you should go; I will counsel you with My eye upon you."

Psalm Therapy -

John 6:29 Jesus replied, "This is the work service that God asks of you: that you believe in the One Whom He has sent that you cleave to, trust, rely on, and have faith in His Messenger." Psalm 84:5 "Blessed happy, fortunate, to be envied is the man whose strength is in You, in whose heart are the highways to The presence and wisdom of the Father."

Psalm Therapy -

There are many things you can focus on and dedicate your life to but the following is the only way that truly works. Psalm 125:1 "Those who TRUST IN, LEAN ON, and CONFIDENTLY CONSISTENTLY HOPE IN THE Living Loving Lord (Father-Jesus-Holy Spirit) are like Mount Zion, which Cannot be Moved but Abides and Stands Fast Forever." Ask The Heavenly Father to help you live this way. There is no better way to live life. Nothing else deserves your full-time focus. Your Father, Jesus and the Holy Spirit are the reason you are alive. If you practice giving your Heart to them every moment of every day, your peace will increase, your joy will destroy depression, love will replace fear and be the hand that comforts and heals, both you and others. The results are amazing, Champion.

Psalm Therapy -

Isaiah 51:3 The Lord says if you Believe and Rejoice in the wilderness, He will make it like Eden, and make your desert like the garden of the Lord. Good News Champion! Your Heavenly Father has a good plan for you - a Promise Land- but there is only one way to get there. --Psalm 95:1-11- "O come, let us sing to the Lord; let us make a joyful noise to the Rock of our salvation! Let us come before His presence with thanksgiving; let us make a joyful noise to Him with songs of praise! For the Lord is a Great God, and a Great King- Above all gods. In His hand are the deep places of the earth; the heights and strength of the hills are His also. The sea is His, for He made it; and His hands formed the dry land. O come, let us worship and bow down, let us kneel before the Lord our Maker in reverent praise and supplication. For He is our God and We are the people of His pasture and the sheep of His hand. TODAY, if you will hear His voice, Harden not your hearts as at Meribah and as at Massah in the day of temptation in the wilderness, When your fathers tried My patience and tested Me, proved Me, and saw My work of judgment. Forty years long was I grieved and disgusted with that generation, and I said, It is a people that do ERR in their hearts, and they DO NOT approve, acknowledge, or regard MY ways. Wherefore I swore in My wrath that they would not enter My rest- the land of promise." Grateful - thankful - faithful - fruitful - JOYFUL! -The Lord says resentment and jealousy must go or you will die in the wilderness. Rejoicing produces Joy, resentment causes bitterness and jealousy causes judgment.

Psalm Therapy -

Psalm 63:7-8 "For You have been my help, and in the shadow of Your wings will I rejoice. My Whole Being Follows Hard after You and Clings closely to You; Your right hand upholds me." Champion, you were never called to work hard. You were called to "Follow Hard". So ask your Heavenly Father to help you and hard will become easy – greased by His amazing grace.

DECEMBER 5

Psalm Therapy -

Champion, you will be Blessed and a Blessing if you (Proverbs 3:5-8) "Lean on, trust in, and be confident in the Lord with All your heart and mind and do not rely on your own insight or understanding. In all your ways; know, recognize, and acknowledge Him, and He will direct and make straight and plain your paths. Be not wise in your own eyes; reverently fear and worship the Lord and turn entirely away from the evil Voice of unbelief – doubt and fear. This way of life leads to health to your nerves and sinews, and marrow and moistening to your bones."

Psalm Therapy -

Champion, what you DWELL ON determines what you DWELL IN-- Psalm 91:1-2 "He who dwells in the shelter of the Most High Will remain secure and rest in the shadow of the Almighty whose power no enemy can withstand. I Will Say of the Lord, "He is my refuge and my fortress, My God, in whom I trust with great confidence, and on whom I rely!". What you are thinking and saying Determines your dwelling place. Do you have Real Peace or are you anxious? You are either Dwelling in peace or anxiety based on your thoughts and words. The Lord says if you Set Your Mind on Me (my faithfulness, my integrity, my ability, my promises), you will dwell in peace.

Champion,

Living in the Lord's Perspective, Champion - it produces hope, strength, peace, joy, power, wisdom, clarity, confidence and courage. It will keep you glad, instead of mad and sad. Ask Him to help you live according to His perspective, then the strategies of Satan will not succeed against you.

Psalm 97:10 "You who love the Lord, hate evil! He protects the lives of his godly people and rescues them from the power of the wicked."

Champion,

The Lord says -"No matter what you've done, someone Loves you more than anyone and That is Me and My Father, if you say YES to My love for you everyday. I will break every chain of shame guilt and condemnation and deliver you from every flavor of fear. I will heal your heart and I will heal your mind and I will give you peace that passes understanding. I will give you joy that nothing else can provide and courage to conquer. "I Love you" really means, "I Love you". " You are valuable" and "You are important to me". "I have a good plan for you and I will bring it to pass because "I Love you","I will not leave you hanging. I will not reject you. I will not abandon you." "I mean what I say and say what I mean". "You can trust my integrity." "I am the Greatest Champion". Forever yours, Jesus

Galatians 5:1 [Freedom in Christ] "So Christ has truly set us free. Now make sure that you stay free, and don't get tied up again in slavery to the law."

Champion,

Zephaniah 3:17 Yahweh, your God, is IN the Midst of You, a Mighty One who will save. He will rejoice over you with joy. He will calm you in His love. Champion, the more you remember and soak in the facts of what He has already done for you, the more you will realize that provision is not a problem and peace will consume your heart. Faith will be fully alive. Stand up and say "No" to the spirit of fear and declare, "my God is near." Jesus left his comfort zone and manifested the Father's love in all He did. He yielded to a horrific death for you and I and rose on the third day and is alive in Heaven. He then sent His Spirit to help us. Meditate on those facts today!

Zephaniah 3:17 "For the Lord your God is living among you. He is a mighty savior. He will take delight in you with gladness. With his love, he will calm all your fears. He will rejoice over you with joyful songs."

Champion,

Mark 14:36 At the time of Jesus's greatest struggle He cried out to God- Abba, which means Father-Dad, everything is possible for You. The work of the Holy Spirit, which is the Spirit of adoption, is to help you receive God, The Heavenly Father, as Your personal Heavenly Dad that loves, listens and will lift You, not Let You down. The strategy of satan is to keep you from that revelation, because if you have that, fear will never be an issue and peace that passes understanding will be your reality. Then the power of God will flow through you like never before.

Mark 14:36 "Abba, Father," he cried out, "everything is possible for you. Please take this cup of suffering away from me. Yet I want your will to be done, not mine."

Champion,

Talk to Him. Draw near with thanksgiving and praise. Exercise your faith and you will recognize how true the following scriptures are: Isaiah 46:4 "Even to your old age I am He, And even to your advanced old age I will carry you! I have made you, and I will carry you; Be assured I will carry you and I will save you. Isaiah 54:10 "For the mountains may be removed and the hills may shake, But My loving kindness will not be removed from you, Nor will My covenant of peace be shaken," says the Lord who has compassion on you. Matthew 28:20b "I am with you always remaining with you perpetually—regardless of circumstance, and on every occasion, even to the end of the age."

Psalm 100:4 "Enter his gates with thanksgiving; go into his courts with praise. Give thanks to him and praise his name."

Champion,

Psalm 139:23-24 says, "Search me thoroughly, O God, and know my heart! Try me and know my thoughts! And see if there is any wicked or hurtful way in me, and lead me in the way everlasting." Take this serious Champion-I have made too many mistakes out of hurt. Hurting hearts effect every area of our lives. Pay attention regularly and ask the Father to deliver you from every wicked or hurtful way. Healthy heart hygiene is critical. Every time you wash your hands or take a shower, wash your heart. Ask God to help you. The inside is more important so you don't bite someone, chew and spit someone out, spreading the hurt. This is a must. We are accountable and will be rewarded or will experience more loss if we do not take this serious. Ask your Father to help you not have a constipated Soul, a heart backed up with frustration, disappointment, and aggravation. Instead, may it be filled with everlasting love and wisdom. Pursue peace, not denial. Ask God to help you.

Psalm 139:23-24 "Search me, O God, and know my heart; test me and know my anxious thoughts. Point out anything in me that offends you, and lead me along the path of everlasting life."

Champion,

LOSS MULTIPLIES. If you do not get healed from loss, the pain, the hurt, fear, anger, unbelief, and doubt will cause you to do things that produce more loss. The blow to your heart, if left unhealed and unfilled with new love and wisdom, will be contaminated with unbelief, doubt, and fear. The strategy of Satan is that loss multiplies in your life and IT WILL unless you say, "No!" based on the truth of scripture.

Psalm 55:22 "Give your burdens to the LORD, and he will take care of you. He will not permit the godly to slip and fall."

Champion,

If you are a believer: born again, saved, a child of God, and if you are one that has said Jesus Christ is Lord, the supreme authority, and I declare Him Lord of my life and love Him back by following Him and learning to do what He says to do, then you have an assurance plan. It is backed by a company with an A+ rating-Father, Son, and Holy Spirit. Romans 8:28 says all things work together for good for those that love God -hear, follow and do what He is saying, believe what He has said, trust and exercise faith in His leadership, and His words. Then it's like a natural insurance company when you yield to their policies, file your claim and receive redemption from your losses. But if you blame the insurance company for the loss instead of going to them for vindication and help to recover from the loss, you never receive help. You don't have a testimony of their faithfulness. Let God show you His faithfulness.

Matthew 11:28 "Then Jesus said, "Come to me, all of you who are weary and carry heavy burdens, and I will give you rest."

Champion,

Satan causes you, in your weakest point of heartache, which comes from suffering loss or things not working out the way you thought they would, to blame God. He does this by twisting the truth and saying, "If God was so good, then why did this happen?" This keeps you from filing your paperwork with your assurance company by faith. It keeps you from drawing near to the throne of grace, going to the Heavenly Father and saying, "You said all things would work together for good for me and I'm really hurting and I really need help. Please prove to me that something good will come out of this. I put my hope and trust in you and your integrity. I refuse to separate myself from the One that died for me and lives to help me." When you do not separate from God and His people, or just go through the motions that look like faith, but go to Him with your broken heart fractured by disappointments, you will see the reality of His goodness. And what was sent against you to destroy you and your faith in Him will cause greater faith in Him. And what the devil sent to destroy your relationship with God will strengthen it.

Psalm 34:18 "The LORD is close to the brokenhearted; he rescues those whose spirits are crushed."

Champion,

To have a strong faith muscle that causes great victories, you must exercise it. And if you exercise it in the hardest times, you will have very strong faith in your Heavenly Father. Don't blame the one that already took the blame for your sin on the cross, or you will never fully recover, and loss will continue to multiply in your life. God never abandons people. It's only people that abandon God out of their wrong thinking when weakened by loss. Whether a little disappointment or large, draw near my friends. He will hear and you will taste and see amazing grace.

James 4:8 "Come close to God, and God will come close to you. Wash your hands, you sinners; purify your hearts, for your loyalty is divided between God and the world."

Champion,

Dress for success! Wondering what to wear today? Something becoming? Would you like to look good, Champion? Be stunning? Make a difference? Do the profitable thing? Wear the outfit that looks the best on you? Represent your Heavenly Father with excellence? Destroy the spirit of heaviness? Be a magnet for God's presence? Be inhabited by God? Experience abundant life? Then here it is, Psalm 33:1 Rejoice in the Lord, O you uncompromisingly righteous you upright in right standing with God; for PRAISE is BECOMING and appropriate for those who are upright in heart. Put on the garment of praise, it destroys the spirit of heaviness. Complaining increases the spirit of heaviness. Isaiah 61:3. God inhabits the praises of His people and without His presence you will not be beautiful, powerful, or wise no matter what else you do. He is the ultimate answer for every good thing.

Psalm 33:1 "Let the godly sing for joy to the LORD; it is fitting for the pure to praise him."

Isaiah 61:3 "To all who mourn in Israel, he will give a crown of beauty for ashes, a joyous blessing instead of mourning, festive praise instead of despair. In their righteousness, they will be like great oaks that the LORD has planted for his own glory."

Champion,

An attitude of gratitude and praise gets me into the throne-room of grace and keeps me there all day long; the secret place , the presence of God, where fullness of joy is found. If you are missing joy or peace, you are not abiding in the truth that sets and keeps you free. Think correctly, it causes you to be grateful, thankful, faithful, and flowing with praise; Energized, healthy, and strong. Think; meditate on, the Heavenly Father's integrity and promises, kindness and generosity. Remember, when you did not deserve it He gave Jesus and His Holy Spirit, the perfect and good gifts, and made you an heir of the most royal family at the moment you put your faith in Him and Jesus. So don't stop believing. Continue to exercise your faith every moment. Rejoice in the midst of foolishness! Ask the Father to help you. Thankfulness and praise keeps you cleansed and filled with the goodness of God.

Philippians 4:8 "And now, dear brothers and sisters, one final thing. Fix your thoughts on what is true, and honorable, and right, and pure, and lovely, and admirable. Think about things that are excellent and worthy of praise."

It's Time, Champion,

Isaiah 60:1 Arise from the depression and prostration in which circumstances and thoughts have kept you—rise to a new life! Shine, be radiant with the glory of the Lord, for your light has come, and the glory of the Lord has risen upon you! Every day we have a choice to believe the word of God or the words of our world, past or present circumstances. Choose life, my friend. Ask God to help you rise to a new life and keep rising. Jesus did not die for you or me, for us, to wallow or swallow, (just accepting things as they are). But stand up and say, "The glory of the Lord, the very presence of God, is with me and for me. Jesus is inside of me and I will honor Him today by agreeing with Him and saying I have been favored by God and I will continue to be. For the Lord is my shepherd and His goodness pursues me and overtakes me, no matter what I see, this is what I will say. I call those things that are not as though they were--just like my Heavenly Father." Rom.4:17.

Isaiah 60:1 "Arise, Jerusalem! Let your light shine for all to see. For the glory of the LORD rises to shine on you."

Proverbs meditation -

The selfish man quarrels against every sound principle of conduct by demanding his own way. A rebel doesn't care about the facts. All he wants to do is yell. A wise man's words express deep streams of thought. A fool gets into constant fights. His mouth is his undoing! His words endanger him. Pride (causing him to be unteachable), ends in destruction. Humility ends in honor. Those who love to talk will suffer the consequences. Men have died for saying the wrong thing!" Champion, ask God to clean you out and fill you up with good stuff so good stuff comes out of your mouth and you are a blessing and not going about messing, like an untrained dog, and stinking up the place.

Proverbs 18:1-2 "Unfriendly people care only about themselves; they lash out at common sense. Fools have no interest in understanding; they only want to air their own opinions."

Proverbs 18:4 "Wise words are like deep waters; wisdom flows from the wise like a bubbling brook."

Proverbs 18:6 "Fools' words get them into constant quarrels; they are asking for a beating."

Proverbs 18:12 "Haughtiness goes before destruction; humility precedes honor."

Proverbs 18:21 "The tongue can bring death or life; those who love to talk will reap the consequences."

Champion,

GOOD NEWS! There is no enemy that can stop the goodness of God if we believe. The greatest enemy is unbelief. It is worse than cancer. So be encouraged by the following testimony of someone that believed, then put your under armor of praise on and thank Him for who He is and making a way for you today as you believe, hear, and obey. Psalm 66:3-6 Say to God, How awesome and fearfully glorious are Your works! Through the greatness of Your power shall Your enemies submit themselves to You -with fake and reluctant obedience. All the earth shall bow down to You and sing praises to You; they shall praise Your name in song. Selah pause, and calmly think of that! Come and see the works of God; see how to save His people He smites their foes; He provides for-defends and avenges His people - He turned the sea into dry land, they crossed through the river on foot; there did we rejoice in Him.

Psalm 66:3-6 "Say to God, "How awesome are your deeds! Your enemies cringe before your mighty power. Everything on earth will worship you; they will sing your praises, shouting your name in glorious songs."

Friend,

The Lord says it's better to experience the pain of correction than the pain of misdirection. The purpose of the Holy Spirit speaking truth that corrects is so we can experience more of His goodness and have more of an impact; a more fulfilling life. Proverbs 12:1 "Whoever loves instruction and correction loves knowledge" (because of the new freedom and prosperity that it brings when applied) but he who hates reproof is like a brute beast, stupid and indiscriminating. Job 5:17 "Happy and fortunate is the man whom God reproves; so do not despise or reject the correction of the Almighty."

Proverbs 12:1 "To learn, you must love discipline; it is stupid to hate correction."

Job 5:17 "But consider the joy of those corrected by God! Do not despise the discipline of the Almighty when you sin."

Champion,

The Bible is a treasure map. The Holy Spirit is the guide to the treasure. Jesus is the door to the treasure. The Father God is the treasure. Seek and you will find the treasure that is greater and more beneficial than any other treasure.

Jeremiah 29:13 "If you look for me wholeheartedly, you will find me."

Champion,

Christmas wisdom: Everyone's heart is like a bank account: you are either depositing into it or withdrawing from it. Make more deposits than withdrawals and things will go well for you. We honor Jesus this Christmas, whose birth we celebrate, who made the greatest deposit imaginable - Eternal Love and Life!

Luke 12:34 "Wherever your treasure is, there the desires of your heart will also be."

Champion,

Christmas is here because God gave His best, His own Son Jesus, and made You His Highest Priority. Let's ask Him to help us give our best and to make Him our Highest Priority! Honoring Him, revering him and bringing Him pleasure in all that we do and all that we say, doing what's right in His sight more and more every day by His Spirit, not our strength. Pursuing this lifestyle produces great rewards that He wants you to experience and it helps others experience His Goodness, which should be your second priority. Merry Christmas.

Galatians 2:20 "My old self has been crucified with Christ. It is no longer I who live, but Christ lives in me. So I live in this earthly body by trusting in the Son of God, who loved me and gave himself for me."

Champion,

Truth spoken in love, that is instruction and correction, can be like vegetables. Even though people are hungry and need nourishment, they stop eating, (receiving), the truth that would create new health and prosperity. Ask God to help you, Champion, and pray for others so we don't miss out on His goodness.

Proverbs 3:12 "For the LORD corrects those he loves, just as a father corrects a child in whom he delights."

DECEMBER 27

Champion,

Here comes a high-protein breakfast only for people that want to be strong and overcome. When you are ungrateful, complaining, you are unfaithful. And when you are unfaithful, you are not a faithful Champion, so you will lose what you have already been given and create your own lack because of your lack of appreciation. Complaining is unfaithfulness. It is a fearful, wicked, lazy attitude and leads to more loss. If this is you or somebody you know, cry out for deliverance because you or they have one of the worst diseases that exists-ungratefulness. UNEXPRESSED thankfulness is ungratefulness. If you look for the good, reasons to praise, you will be constantly thankful and constantly faithful and you will be given more of God's goodness.

Psalm 100:4 "Enter his gates with thanksgiving; go into his courts with praise. Give thanks to him and praise his name."

Champion,

When your highest priority is bringing the Lord honor, bringing Him pleasure by your attitude and actions, then nothing else matters. No disappointment, no injustice , no fear of loss or suffering of any kind--nothing can or will stop you from being and doing all that He's called you to be and do. You will have an amazing life making the difference that you were created to make by His Spirit if you persevere in faith. Ask the Father to help you!

Isaiah 25:1 "O LORD, I will honor and praise your name, for you are my God. You do such wonderful things! You planned them long ago, and now you have accomplished them."

Champion,

On this day, you will experience the divine if you take some time and honor and praise the living God for the many flavors of His excellent nature. He will honor you for honoring Him and The following Psalm will be your legacy--

Psalm 92:12-15 "The uncompromisingly righteous shall flourish like the palm tree be long-lived, stately, upright, useful, and fruitful; they shall grow like a cedar in Lebanon majestic, stable, durable, and incorruptible. Planted in the house of the Lord, they shall flourish in the courts of our God. Growing in grace they shall still bring forth fruit in old age; they shall be full of sap of spiritual vitality and rich in the verdure of trust, love, and contentment. They are living memorials to show that the Lord is upright and faithful to His promises; He is my Rock, and there is no unrighteousness in Him."

Champion,

Put on the under armor of praise on and you will Triumph through Jesus Christ. 2Cor 2:14 "and you will have strength and wisdom to do all things that you need to do", "through Christ who strengthens you." Phil.4:13.

Psalm 84:4-7 expresses this... Blessed, happy, fortunate, to be envied are those who dwell in Your house and Your presence; Who think about the reality of who you are and what you have already done -they will be singing Your praises all the day. Blessed happy, fortunate, to be envied is the man whose strength comes from you- because they are constantly relying on your ability to help them. Passing through the Valley of Weeping (Baka), they make it a place of springs; the early rain also fills the pools with blessings. They go from strength to strength increasing in victorious power; each of them experiencing the power of your presence as they praise you-transforming the place of sorrow into the place of joy-watching strongholds of the enemy come down as they continue to praise you – putting all their hope and faith in you.

Psalm 84:4-7 "What joy for those who can live in your house, always singing your praises. What joy for those whose strength comes from the Lord, who have set their minds on a pilgrimage to Jerusalem. When they walk through the Valley of Weeping, it will become a place of refreshing springs. The autumn rains will clothe it with blessings. They will continue to grow stronger,"

Champion,

Guarantees are only as good as the Guarantor, the one that makes the Promise. So if God says Humility and Reverence for Him produces life, honor and provision, then it will!! Because of His integrity and ability, it will come to pass. He says what He means and means what He says. Come out of double mindedness and into the Power of single-mindedness. You will have a Happy New Year if you stand fast on this Wisdom. It's Time to come out of the hurt of what you have not seen God do and proclaim His promises. It's time to stop being afraid and rejoice with a new song... *"There is nothing that I need that God will not supply!"* "He already gave His best, He'll give me the rest that I need." "Even more than I can think or imagine. " "Even the desires of my heart." "Even the fullness of His good plan will manifest in my life". Stand tall my friend and enter this new year with the Roar of a Lion!

Numbers 28:19-20 *"God is not a man, so he does not lie. He is not human, so he does not change his mind. Has he ever spoken and failed to act? Has he ever promised and not carried it through? Listen, I received a command to bless; God has blessed, and I cannot reverse it!"*

ABOUT THE AUTHOR

 Dr. Edgar "Skip" Gunn is the senior pastor of Life Church in Hampden, Massachusetts. He is called as an apostolic father and has served many in the Springfield area for decades. Skip's prophetic instinct and Holy Spirit led daily life make him a highly valued part of the discipleship of many. His personal testimony of deliverance from fear and rejection have brought hope and freedom to thousands.

Skip & his wife, Diane, are the co-founders of New Life International Ministries, Inc.(1990), The Destiny Center (2002) and The Institute of Vision, Purpose & Destiny (2011), where the body of Christ in New England can grow and be nurtured in their walk with Christ. He is also the founder and president of Nehemiah Community Development Corp., an organization dedicated to community transformation.

Skip and Diane Gunn have been happily married since 1978. They have three children and eight grandchildren. All of their children are involved in leadership and using their gifts for the Body of Christ.

RESOURCES AND RECOMMENDED LINKS

FAITH - www.LivingByFaithBlog.com

PROMISES-www.WhatChristiansWantToKnow.com

www.intouch.org/you/gods-promises

www.365promises.com/

GRATITUDE -www.HappierHuman.com/benefits-of-gratitude

ENCOURAGING BIBLE VERSES http://www.jollynotes.com

NAMES OF GOD - http://ldolphin.org/names.html

BIBLE STUDIES - http://www.milk2solidfood.com

RECOMMENDED BOOKS-

"*SWITCH ON YOUR BRAIN*" -Dr. Caroline Leaf
"*THE EVERYDAY GUIDE TO PRAYER*" -Julia Quinn
"DESTINED TO REIGN" -Joseph Prince
"CREATE YOUR WORLD" -Patricia King

TO SUBSCRIBE TO SKIP'S TEXT CHAMPIONS HOTLINE
EMAIL SKIP AT ChampionsPlaybook@gmail.com

49198879R00207

Made in the USA
Charleston, SC
17 November 2015